Praise for *Russian Roulette*

How do we unravel the Gordian (Gorkian?) Knot of contemporary Russia and its relation to the rest of the world, especially the West? Suppose we could revive some of Russia's greatest authors, who were at the same time her most serious critics, and transport them to today. Imagine Turgenev applying his inescapable grounding in family and the freight of history. How would Dostoyevsky play the psychologist of a world, somewhat his own, somewhat foreign, a century and a half after his time? Follow Gogol's eye for the absurd into times more inane than he could have imagined. Put that into language to rival Chekov's unmatched lyricism. These are the tissues of Victor Pogostin's novel. Add to it deep currents of intrigue and suspense that would make Robert Ludlum jealous, and you have Russian Roulette.

Ron Cooper, Professor of Philosophy at College of Central Florida and author of *Hume's Fork*

The Soviet Union may have imploded more than four decades ago, but the men at the helm of Russia today were all born and bred in the USSR. These exemplars of what the Soviet State once proudly called the New Soviet Man, are the products of a system, which, while avowing equal rights for all, fostered inequalities, bred cynicism, and propagated a survivalist mentality, whereby personal good was to be pursued at all costs, with a blatant disregard for everyone else. If you want an insight into the inner world of these men—if you want to understand what living in that system looked like in practice—you should look no further than Victor Pogostin's book of darkly funny and keenly observed non-fiction stories of life in both Soviet and post-Soviet Russia. Pogostin, once a Moscow intellectual and a privileged translator (he translated the works of Ernest Hemingway into Russian), had a unique position both inside and outside of the Soviet system, before his emigration to Canada in the late 1990s. The wildly entertaining stories he tells in the book, all written in a muscular and energetic English, bear testimony to the many absurdities, tragicomedies, and frustrations that formed the fabric of everyday life and of human relations both in the Soviet Union and in what came after it.

> Maria Bloshteyn, author of *Russia is Burning: Poems of the Great Patriotic War*

Victor Pogostin's insight into Russian life – REAL Russian life – in the Soviet Union and how the "Iron Curtain" remnants still influence and impact Russia today is unsurpassed in his book "Russian Roulette." As an American, I found his highly relatable style of storytelling put me right there with him as he busted many misconceptions I embraced about life in Russian; grinding the bones of the modern mythology I trusted while explaining many of the truths I suspected. From his return to his native soil to deal with the death of his brother to the strangely serendipitous circumstances that finally led to what could compellingly be described as an escape to Canada, Russian expatriate Pogostin's must-read book (and I do not use that term lightly) is for anyone seeking to not just learn and understand, but feel the complications, the hardships, often the abject criminality of Cold War life in the Soviet Union and beyond. I unreservedly recommend this book to you.

> Joe Buonfiglio – Author of *The Post-Apocalyptic Dining Guide*

Victor illuminates what it took to subsist on a daily basis even as an officer in the "Navy Aviation" division. His pathway there is a demonstration of what we perceive Russia to be. And while it may seem quintessentially military, none of that would ever have happened in America. Saving old light bulbs, Stolichnaya as currency, etc. A window into Russian society that is sardonically disturbing, but funny and guiltily entertaining.

> LTC (Dr.) Richard J. Lewis, USAFR Flight Surgeon (Ret.)

RUSSIAN ROULETTE
BY VICTOR POGOSTIN

Blotter Books

Published by The Blotter Magazine, Inc.
Copyright 2021 by Victor Pogostin
First Printing 2021

All rights reserved. No part of this publication may be reproduced, or transmitted in any form or by any means, electronic or mechanical, including photocopying, recording or any information storage and retrieval system, without the written permission of the author.

Pogostin, Victor 1945 -
Russian Roulette
ISBN 978-1-7323938-6-8
Published in the United States by Blotter Books
an imprint of The Blotter Magazine, Inc.
1010 Hale Street, Durham, NC 27705

Cover designed by Olivia Somers
Author photo by George Pogostin

Printed and bound in the USA

VICTOR POGOSTIN

Table of Contents:

Part One – Just So Stories

9	An Expat Goes Home
22	An Alien's Guide to the Subway
25	Russian Roulette in Gorky Park
31	Coffee and Ideological Maxims in Moscow
37	Moths in the Iron Curtain or Roaming in the USSR with Al Purdy and Ralph Gustafson
54	Virgin Lands - Sputniks and Painless Parker
60	Putsch

Part Two – At A Far Meridian

65	Bon Voyage
67	Kasimpur
70	Communist maxims put to test
74	Impromptu break in the cold war
78	Tigers hunt at dawn
83	Appendix
91	Coming home
93	Comrade Major
95	Taking a Train in England – An Adventure

Part Three – Business *A La Russ*

99	Sidewalk business
101	The art of negotiations
104	The road to hell is paved with good intentions
108	Project Lifetime

Part Four – The Bare Necessities

114	Plumbers come twice
117	"A car is not a luxury, but a means of transportation"
120	Black "Volga" an emblem of authority
122	Funny and Poignant
123	The rogues and the villains
128	The two blemishes I kept
130	Back door shopping
132	Butcher-Matador

Part Five – Health care for all

137	Koi pond
141	Panangin

Part Six – Charlie Foxtrot

145	Clusterfuck
151	An Exemplary Garrison
153	Boot Camp
166	Hands off the Epaulets
174	In The Land of The Flawed
180	Autopilot

Part Seven – Disenchantment

189	
211	Passage to Canada

VICTOR POGOSTIN

To my late parents, my understanding wife Natasha, my caring son George, my daughter-in-law Tamara and my wonderful grandchildren David and Victoria who may read this book when they grow up.

Part One - Just so Stories

An Expat Goes Home

At dawn one day in late November, I was awakened by a call. It was my niece, sobbing: "Uncle Vic... Papa died."

My elder brother Vladimir had died in the subway on the way to work. A Moscow policeman found his cell phone on him and dialed the first number listed in the contacts. An hour later, an email from the Research Institute, where my brother worked his entire professional life, confirmed his death.

Visiting one's home country after a long

absence (I left in 1993) might seem like a thrill but be careful what you wish for. Changes can leave you with a sickening nostalgia for lost memories, while making places and events from one's past, once so dear, seem like nothing but hallucinations.

I found that not only had the street names changed, but once sullen, Soviet display windows now challenge shoppers with the glitter of Channel, Armani, Gucci, and the like. And the places that I cherished: the curved side alleys, the inner yards where I grew up playing with friends who are no longer there – those are the changes that hurt the most.

And while change may be a popular word in Moscow; alas, some things never change.

To go to Moscow, I had to get a visa. The email from my brother's place of work produced no effect in the Russian Consulate. "Anyone could have sent this message," said a consulate official who avoided looking me in the face, trying to hide the odor of alcohol on his morning-breath: "A formal telegram is required."

From time immemorial, only the Central Telegraph Office in Moscow had dispatched formal telegrams of this sort. And for that, a sender had to produce an official death certificate.

The next day was Saturday, and the registry office was not issuing certificates.

My brother's friends' so called 'donation' helped to change circumstances, and the telegram was sent; yet it reached Toronto only after my return from Russia.

Lo and behold, four days later I landed in Moscow. A friend offered to meet me at the Sheremetyevo airport. It had been twelve years since we had seen each other, and it was not the changes in his looks that struck me. He had been a devout communist in the Soviet days, now he crossed himself every time we passed a church.

That November, Moscow was bitterly cold. With the wind blowing tiny icicles at my face, my first nostalgic night-stroll ended quickly in the Okhotny Ryad, a new, upscale underground trade center built beneath Manege Square, which separates Tverskaya Street from the Kremlin. I found a coffee house on the main floor, alongside a cozy fountain and a white grand piano. A shop sign invitingly promised, "What else if not a cup of fragrant espresso or delicate cappuccino to cheer you up!"

True, my espresso came, steaming and aromatic, in a fine china cup. And so, I thought, recalling how ten years before getting a cup of coffee in Moscow was not so easy, that some things had changed for the better. Later, already in bed, I watched one of the many propaganda TV talk shows filled with commercials. One in particular caught my attention. It was about "the superior service and caring staff of the Moscow funeral services." Well... I thought falling asleep that at least my brother would be laid to rest with dignity.

The following morning was even colder and snowier than the night before. An old Camry borrowed from a friend, straining and grumbling through the drifts, finally broke through the traffic jam-ups to reach the hospital gate. The barrier at the gate was closed. The guard did not even look at me. "No cars allowed...100 rubles," he muttered in one breath. Tariff announced, I handed two dollars through the window and the barrier opened.

The hospital morgue was squeezed into a small, one-story, grey brick building with no room, not even a restroom, for the waiting relatives and friends.

Four funeral buses were waiting, engines running. Our bus was third in line. In the bus, the heater worked only in the driver's cabin, and my Camry was the only refuge from the cold for a dozen friends who had come to say farewell.

The wait stretched to over an hour, and we all needed a restroom. Next to the morgue was a dilapidated, green-planked wooden structure. I peeped through the frost-covered window, spotted a human silhouette inside and knocked. A tiny vent window opened, and a young woman looked back at me quizzically.

"Excuse me, is this part of the morgue?" I asked.

"Hell no. It's a laboratory"

"Do you have a restroom?"

"Yes, but only for staff."

I squeezed two dollars in the narrow opening.

"Okay but make it quick and your party only."

I signaled to our small group, and one by one we surreptitiously sneaked in and out.

Soon it was our turn in the morgue. A large, red-faced man, wearing a shabby jacket over a soiled green gown, appeared on the morgue porch holding a coffin lid.

"Who'll carry the coffin?" he demanded.

"They are looking for 'a little extra,'" my brother's friend whispered in my ear.

I didn't mind paying extra, but my brother's friends and I thought we should carry it ourselves.

"We will," I said.

He shrugged his shoulders, dropped the lid in the snowdrift alongside the porch and gestured us inside, where we found a small room with concrete walls painted green.

After a nearly ninety-minute drive, chilled to the bone, we arrived at the crematorium attached to Nikolo-Arkhangelskoye Cemetery. Opened in 1974, it now did seventy cremations per day. We had missed our designated time and were put at the back of the line. Fast learner that I am, this time I quickly found the ritual administrator and, thanks to a hefty 'extra,' the waiting line shortened. However, the time for eulogies had to be cut from the designated fifteen minutes to ten.

Following a colleague from the research institute, where my brother worked, and one of my brother's closest friends, it was my turn to say a few words. Suddenly, a sad-looking figure of an Orthodox priest clad in a worn-out robe squeezed his way through the thick crowd and placed an icon at my brother's feet.

"Wait," I said, trying to stop him. "My brother was not only a committed atheist, but he was also Jewish."

My comment ignored, the priest hurriedly muttered the psalm, "Blessed is our Lord God, always now and ever," sprinkled holy water over the coffin, placed a shroud over my brother's face, and then left, giving me no time to say a word.

Outside, the steel-gray clouds opened up, and a bright winter sun cast a long shadow: the crematorium chimney over the dazzling white snow.

"No worries," said my brother's friend, "we'll have a memorial at the Institute, and you'll speak there."

The memorial stretched out to dusk, and I

gladly availed myself of Institute Director's offer to drive me to Donskoy Monastery Cemetery, where a week later the urn with my brother's ashes would be placed in the columbarium niche alongside our parents.

The monastery was founded in 1591, during the rule of Boris Godunov, and closed in 1917 after the Bolshevik revolution. The New Donskoy Cemetery was added to the medieval burial grounds and a crematorium opened in 1927. It was closed for burials in 1980 and any new burial in the columbarium required special permission from the Moscow City Council. The deceased had to have a certain rating in the unwritten list of bureaucratic ranks to be granted such permission. My father had passed away in 1981. He had been the chief engineer of a large energy trust and a brief obituary in Vechernyaya Moskva (Evening Moscow), the official newspaper of the Moscow government, signaled that he should get a family niche.

It was dark when I was dropped off at the cemetery. The narrow door in the pink-hued metal gates was locked. There was no bell, so I pounded on the door hoping to get some attention. Soon I heard squeaky footsteps on snow and a bearded man, his face half-hidden by a fur hat, peered out through the narrow opening.

"What?" he demanded.

"Can you let me in?"

"Can't you read?" He pointed to the hours of operation sign hanging outside the door.

I shoved a twenty-dollar bill through the opening and the heavy door opened. Inside it was dark. Only the bleak, steel-grey moon shed a feeble light on the dusting of snow sprinkled atop the monastery walls, spruce trees, tombstones, and the crematorium tower.

"Have a flashlight?" I asked.

He walked on, gesturing for me to follow him to a small wooden lodge.

Once inside, he took off his hat. In the bright light the bearded face looked strangely familiar.

"Hey," I said. "Do I know you?"

Avoiding looking at me, he reached outside the vent window, grabbed a plastic bag with vodka, filled two not very clean glasses and handed me one.

"Maybe..."

"Jog my memory."

"First Koptelsky Lane - my father was the yard-keeper."

It rang a bell. Our family had lived there for over twenty years, and my brother and I were born there. The yard-keeper was a huge Tatar with a bushy, smoky moustache, and a yellowish, worn-out leather apron.

"Holly Smoke!" I burst out, "Alex?"

We had never been close friends, but he and his Dad had been sort of permanent fixtures in the lives of the inhabitants of the four-building complex where we lived. German architects had designed the building in the 1930s. Architects and engineers from Germany had been invited by Stalin's regime to help with the industrialization of the country. Residents of our gated community presented a fascinating mixture of high-ranking technocrats, government officials, educators, as well as military and security officers.

I still remember the clanking of the chains at dawn's first light when Alex's dad opened the iron gates to let in the Black Raven (a secret police car used to arrest "enemies of the people" during Stalin's Purges). I was in second grade when the "ravens" stopped coming. Then, on the frosty, sunny, early spring morning of March 5, 1953, I looked out the window to see if my buddies were waiting for me to walk to school and saw two strange looking flags, their rich, red cloth framed by black ribbons.

"Look Mom...," I called out.

She did and said only one word in reply: "Stalin."

There were no tears in our family. Yet at our all-boys school classes were cancelled, and all students, from grades one to ten, were lined up in the main hall in front of the huge, full-length portrait of the moustached generalissimo in his high glossy boots. The teachers were crying, some genuinely, others from joy or fear of the unknown times looming.

As for us, first and second graders, we found it hard to stand at attention. We pushed and pinched and giggled. The teachers desperately tried to restrain us. I remember that my elder brother, who was in grade 10 at the time, frowned down at me.

The last time I had seen Alex was many years before. I had run into him on the street. He was only a few weeks out of jail, where he had spent three years for hard currency profiteering.

"Just think! "He gulped his vodka down. "Why are you here?"

"My parents are here, and my brother's urn will join them next week. You?"

"Business. We are taking it over."

"We?"

"Trustworthy guys."

"I see..."

"Like hell you do... Come on, I'll walk you to your niche."

Walking through a cemetery at night is no fun, but in this columbarium, there was a sector that always sent the chills up my spine.

In 1930, the city dug up a large pit that was

then used as a common grave for some victims of Stalin's purges. Two more pits were added later. Over 5000 Muscovites were shot and cremated in Donskoy, their ashes dumped in the pits. In 1989, the Gorbachev Government put up a sign "To the Eternal Memory of the Innocent Victims of Political Repressions."

While I brushed the snow from the ceramic photos on our family's niche, Alex waited at a distance, leaving me alone to my memories.

Back in the shed, he handed me another shot.

"Hungry?"

"No. Just cold."

"Well... I am. Want a steak?"

I looked around – no barbecue. He caught my puzzled look.

"I heard you'd left. Where to?"

"Canada."

"Man, you lucked out there. Come on."

He kicked a small electric grill. "Chinese shit... useless. Check out mine!"

He led me to a large mesh grate made from an old metal bed. The corners of the mesh were attached to electrical wires. He winked at me and plugged it in. In a few minutes, the mesh turned gray and then bright purple. The room warmed up. He took a huge steak from a plastic bag hanging outside the window, threw it on a pan, and started cooking on his DIY grill. The room was filled with the aroma of sizzling meat.

"May your brother rest in peace." He passed me another glass of vodka.

"You still live in our building?"

"Hell no. The city took it over for 'major repairs' and kicked all the residents out to suburbs. They are tougher than us."

"I'd like to go there"

"Why? No one's left."

"David?"

"In Israel."

"Eugene?"

"In Germany."

"Yuri?"

"Killed in Chechnya"

"Misha?"

"In the States."

"Sava?"

"Be damned. He was the one who locked me up. Colonel now."

We had a few more drinks for the road and he offered to drive me.

"Sure?" I asked pointing to the emptied bottle. "What if the police pull you over?"

"You serious?" He chuckled. "Don't fret. We have them covered."

Many things have changed in Moscow, with its

freshly painted and backlit bridges. In May 2016, a huge brawl took place at the Khovansky Cemetery in Moscow, followed by a shootout. It involved between 200 and 400 'trustworthy guys' from rival groups. Several died. This ended the turf war for the Moscow underground funeral services market, which, according to media sources has an annual turnover of between 12 and 14 billion rubles ($180-210 million).

In addition, starting in the second quarter of 2019, the "GBU Ritual" (government funeral services) intends to demolish all open columbaria walls at Donskoy Cemetery. New walls will be built, where the "Ritual" is going to transfer over 63,000 of the old burial niches. At the end of this venture, a "free reserve" of 3,714 columbary niches should be made available for sale. It is unclear what will happen to the niches of those who do not have relatives living in Moscow: who will ensure the transfer of the urns? Would I have to go back, hoping to run into Alex again?

That is, of course, if he wasn't one of the unlucky guys shot in the brawl.

***

VICTOR POGOSTIN

An Alien's Guide to the Subway

If you read in Webster's dictionary that Subway is 'an electric underground railway,' don't take it for granted. Dictionaries are written by language pundits in quiet, softly-lit, and lightly-heated libraries, whose subtle aura offers little, if any, protection from the onslaught of the fast-food jargon.

One of my first trips to North America was to Washington in the mid-1980s. I came with a group of Soviet sociologists invited to the annual convention of the American Sociological Association.

On leaving Moscow, the official parting wishes from the Academy of Sciences were: *be aware of agents' provocateur attempting to lure the Soviet scholars to America.* While those wistful wishes were for the group in general, I had special orders from a higher authority, my wife, to deliver a bag with winter clothing to her friend's husband, Boris, who had recently relocated to the States.

Mindful of *agents-provocateur*, I did not risk calling Boris from the hotel room, and instead stashed the sweaters and woolen socks in a shopping bag, and one night, when the group retired after a long day of imbibing American sociological wisdom, called Boris from an outside pay phone. Boris worked in a garage and suggested we meet that night around ten, by the first southbound car in the nearest Metro station.

"They call it a subway here," he said. "Just walk to 12th Street, turn right, walk half a block, and you'll see the entrance."

I followed his instructions to the letter and there it was – a color neon SUBWAY sign. True, the door and the stairs seemed a little too narrow for a station entrance, but the Americans were certainly entitled to their own ways.

Inside, the narrow room framed by the glass counter ended with a small "staff only" door with no visible passage to the station. Behind the counter there were two men dressed like twins in navy-colored shirts and aprons. For a minute or two, I stood motionless in the middle of the room filled with the aromas of bread, meats and hot cheese. The men behind the counter scrutinized me closely.

"What would you like to eat, sir?"

"Eat? I am looking for the subway entrance." I tried to wipe a puzzled smile off my face and feeling like Pinocchio in search of a hidden door, looked around again. No hidden door.

The clock on the wall behind the counter said five minutes past ten. Boris was probably waiting for me.

"This is the place," said one of the men.

"Chicken parmesan, chicken and bacon ranch, bacon double cheese. We make sandwiches, fresh!"

"I mean the subway station. Metro."

Now it was their turn to puzzle their wits, but I did not wait for an answer.

"Take care!" I tried to sound casual and left.

Outside, it was dark. The streetlights were on, but there were neither other subway signs nor even passersby to ask. I was by myself, alone on the other side of the planet and hated everything from my English instructor to sandwiches and defectors. A police cruiser stopped.

"Anything wrong, sir?"

"Is there a metro station around? You know, underground?"

"You mean the subway."

Not again, I thought, looking over my shoulder at the "all fresh" sandwich store, but the officer pointed in the direction of some not-so-distant lights.

"Not from the neighborhood?"

"Alien," I said, suddenly remembering the word from my visa application form.

"Yeah," he smiled. "Hop in. I'll give you a ride."

***

Russian Roulette at Gorky Park

In 1993, shortly before my wife and I moved to Canada, our plans were nearly destroyed by a personal encounter with Russia's crime wave.

The day was hot and to thwart pickpockets I thought it would be safer to stash my wallet in my wife's locked handbag than carry it in my back pocket. We had been pushing and shoving at department stores for hours, looking for a new suit for me to take on the trip. No suit could be found, but at the end of the day we came across an Austrian winter overcoat in a small store nearby.

My wife opened her locked purse to pay for the purchase, only to find that my wallet had disappeared.

Gone also were our passports with visas for Canada and my driving license that I foolishly kept with my wallet. My money, of course, had vanished as well.

We searched the car. We remembered back all the places we had been during the day. My wife was sure she had never opened her locked bag until the Austrian overcoat became available. Obviously, someone had opened it for her.

Since the passports and visas could never be replaced in a month's time, which was all the time we had, we couldn't possibly take the trip. We returned home empty handed and defeated.

An hour later, the phone rang. My wife answered, and by the frightened look on her face I knew the call was for me. It was a man with a heavy Caucasian accent - to a Muscovite, a trademark of the criminal underworld.

"Lost anything today?" The voice came from a public telephone; I could hear street noises in the background.

"My wallet, "I said, trying with difficulty to sound indifferent.

"Suppose I have it, " the man said. " What would you pay to get it back? "

"Well, you can have the money that was in it."

I thought that was very generous. The money I had for my new suit was well above the average monthly salary in Moscow.

"Kidding!" the man laughed. "There was no money in your wallet. I want $1,500 U.S." At the time this was about thirty times the salary of a Russian PhD.

"No way," I told him, and I meant it. "I don't have that much money. And it'll take me a few weeks to get it."

"Come on," he chuckled. "Look at your business card. You must be doing a lot of travelling abroad, so you have to have money. Here is my last offer: find a thousand, and I'll give you four hours to do it. I'll meet you later tonight, 11 o'clock at the entrance to the Novodevichy Convent (*a famous cemetery in Moscow, located next to the 16th-century Monastery*). Come alone. And no tricks."

I needed the travel documents badly but meeting those guys - I thought there must be more than one - was worse than having a blind date after midnight in Central Park, in pre-Giuliani New York.

"Why not at the cemetery?"

My caller chuckled again. We finally agreed to meet near a bookstore, not far from a well-lit entrance to the Gorky Park subway station.

"I have to go, " I told her and my worried 12-year-old-son. " All our plans for going to Canada are at stake."

I started to think about it some more: $100 was all the U.S. cash I had in the apartment. But even if I could get more, I did not want those guys to think I could, or I would never get them off my back.

I tried to calm my wife's fears, by finding a friend, as back up, but on a warm Saturday night they all seemed to be out of town.

Then I remembered: When burglars had broken into our apartment the previous year and the police arrived fifty minutes after getting the apartment's alarm signal, explaining that there was no patrol car available, a police Captain, a nice guy, promised to call me if there was any news about stolen property.

I called him now. He remembered me and although sounded as sympathetic as he had last year, he couldn't leave the police station or provide me with an officer to drive with me.

"Don't go," he said. "You are liable to get knocked on the head and you'll lose your car too. Try to make them agree to meet you on Monday and I may have someone to watch your back."

I was on my own. I dug out an old starter's pistol used at track meets I'd picked up somewhere. And I took along a new crispy $100 U.S. bank note. After all, the man on the phone sounded like he was in a negotiating mood.

The bookstore was located on a wide public avenue, but there weren't that many people around at that time of night. I parked a few yards from the sidewalk, leaving the motor running. I eyed the few pedestrians that passed by with suspicion. They must have wondered about me. I watched passing cars like a hawk. An hour went by. No one. Midnight and still no one, not even a lonely policeman.

I thought I'd smoke another pipe and then leave. Just as I was tamping the tobacco, a red Lada (a Russian car model based on the Italian FIAT-124 sedan) stopped beside me, so close I couldn't open my door on the driver's side. Two guys - just something about them, I knew. It was dark and I couldn't see their faces well. The guy in the passenger seat rolled down his window and in the light of the streetlamp I could only see that he had a dark brown mustache and the guy behind the wheel had a black and coal beard. The guy in the passenger seat asked directions to the Gorky Park.

"If you have my wallet, no need to go anywhere," I said.

"How do we know you are alone?" the man said. "Drive around the corner. You go first and we'll follow."

I turned around the corner and stopped the car.

The red Lada again pulled in so close to my door that I was a prisoner on that side of the car.

"Brought the money?" the man said, showing me my wallet. He looked like a thug. They both did.

I showed him my crisp $100 bill.

"That's all I could get."

"Fuck you. Look for your wallet in the river." And he made a motion of throwing it a long way out in imaginary, nearby water. Then gears clashed and the Lada dashed away.

Well, I was wrong about them settling for less. But I didn't feel very philosophical about it, thinking of my now aborted trip to Canada. Then out of nowhere they came back.

"You're fucking lucky," the man said. "We haven't got time to play around. Let's do it."

"Show me the papers that were in the wallet," I said, my confidence regained.

He turned the dome light on and lifted my wallet and papers high enough for me to see them. Then with one hand, he slowly extended them toward me.

I reached out toward him with my $100 bill, slowly and distrustfully. Just as our right hands neared each other in the space between the two cars, we both made a sudden grab with our left hands. Then the Lada roared away.

My wife was in tears when I got home, and my son had a butcher knife in his hand.

"I thought you might be in the Moscow River, or you were being tortured somewhere," my wife said.

"And my murderers were about to come crashing through the doorway..." Now it was my turn to chuckle. I called the friendly policeman.

"You did it and are back. " He sounded matter-of-fact. "You are a lucky guy."

***

RUSSIAN ROULETTE

Coffee and Ideological Maxims in Moscow

Coffee in Moscow may be as good as anywhere else, but did you ever try to buy it in the same bar of the same hotel, and yet in two different countries and even in different epochs? Well, I did.

On the eve of the May Day — 'International Day of Workers' Solidarity' — festivities I, like thousands of fellow Muscovites, was awakened by the bravura songs praising the symbiosis and the achievements of the proletariat, the working intelligentsia and the collective farmers and set out on what we called the 'gastronomic adventure.' This was a euphemism, not to be confused with consuming delicacies, for ransacking the city food stores in search of food.

When the dusty sunset was closing in on the city, I felt exhausted. The day was nearing its end and so were Gorbachev's perestroika of the early '90s and the scarce supply of food in Moscow stores. Coffee was no exception. Having failed to buy it in the stores, I figured I could get it at a hotel bar. The 'Intourist' hotel stood at the very mouth of Gorky Street, towering over the Kremlin and the city center like an obscene middle finger amidst two- and three-storied 19th century buildings housing an old 'National' hotel, decorated with a natural stone, stucco and marble façade and stained-glass windows on the one side, and a two-story-with-amezzanine mansion, now the theatre named after the famous dramatic actress Maria Yermolova, on the other.

The communist maxim insisted: 'From each according to his ability, to each according to his needs.' Well, I certainly had both, the need and the ability to enjoy a cup of strong coffee. The hotel bar was in the front lobby and, after passing through a close order of heavily built and slightly tipsy doorkeepers; I made my way to a high stool by the bar counter. While the bartender worked on the coffee machine, I lit my pipe and prepared to enjoy my espresso. It finally came, steaming and aromatic, in a delicate china cup. To save time on getting the bartender's attention, I offered to pay for it right away.

"Dollar-fifty." The bartender did not even look in my direction, consumed as he was by the other more prospective liquor-ordering customers.

"And in rubles?"

"We don't accept rubles here. It's a hard-currency bar." (That is, a place where customers paid only hard currency, like US dollars.)

I turned around, for the first-time paying attention to the visitors—a good sprinkling of hard-currency clients—and realized I was in a 'foreigner's only' establishment. In the Soviet Union, there were plenty of the sort - bars, restaurants, supermarkets, even clothes stores restricted to the Russians and servicing the hard-currency tourists and a small diplomatic and western business community.

"How about fifteen rubles?" I tried. With the black-market price at about six rubles for a dollar, I figured he wouldn't resist. But the spoiled brat was intent on teaching me a lesson.

"Dollar fifty." I bet I saw him grin.

"Well, then, take it back." And he did. The steaming, aromatic cup went straight into the bar's sink. At least one of the communist maxims proved wrong.

Six years later my work assignment brought me to Moscow. This time, I was traveling with a Canadian passport. Change was in the air in Russia. True enough, the Soviet Union was dissolved, perestroika was long forgotten, and the night news commentator was talking about war in Chechnya, investments in Moscow Realty and Mediterranean cruises and the Rotary Club in Russia.

Even the 'International Day of Worker's Solidarity' was now called the 'Day of Celebration of Spring and Labor.'

Change or no change, the 'Intourist' was still there. Heavily built and heavily tipsy security guards now reinforced the slightly tipsy doorkeepers. I checked in on the night ending the 'Spring and Labor' festivities. Out of my 20th floor window, the former Gorky Street now renamed Tverskaya, the restored 'National' hotel now called Le Royal Meridien National, the Ermolova Theatre, the old Moscow University buildings and the Kremlin lay down below, with rainbow reflections from the huge neon ads splashed on the green roofs, wet from rain.

I felt excited anticipating new encounters with the familiar yet changed places in my home city, but it was late and there were several family visits planned for me the next day. Having quenched my excitement with a triple scotch, I called for a 7 am wake-up call and coffee to the room, watched the news frequently interrupted by ads offering imported delicacies and even organic coffee, and went to bed.

A heavy knock on my door awakened me at about 7:30 am. Through a peephole I saw one of the security guards.

"What happened?" I asked in English.

"Time, Sir," said my wake-up call and slowly walked back to the elevator. My coffee never came. Well, some 20 floors down there was the still-not-forgotten front lobby bar, and this time I was one of the privileged hard-currency holders.

The bar was there all right. Even the bartender looked very much like the other guy six years ago. I made my way to a high stool by the counter. While the bartender worked on the coffee machine, I lit my pipe and prepared to enjoy my espresso. It came, steaming and aromatic, in a plastic disposable cup. To save time on getting the bartender's attention, I offered to pay for it right away.

"How much?"

"Hundred and fifty rubles."

"And in dollars?"

"No dollars here. It's Moscow."

"I know," I said. "I was born here."

"We all were." I bet I saw him grin.

I looked around. The scenery was the same, only the visitors different—a good sprinkling of new rich sipping morning Champagne, some with their pre-money wives, others with their post-money mistresses. Something did change after all, and the bartender made an effort to be helpful.

"You can change your dollars in a bank. It's just around the corner."

"Can I bill it to my room?"

"Sorry, it is 'cash only' bar."

"Take it back then." And he did.

The steaming, aromatic cup went straight into the bar's sink.

Well, this time a Rotarian maxim 'Service Above Self—He Profits Most Who Serves Best' failed in the new Russia.

I heard recently the 'Intourist' hotel was pulled

down. I may soon be back in Moscow and who knows what ideological maxim I might see fail this time. I have quite a few to test. After all, nothing ventured, nothing gained.

***

RUSSIAN ROULETTE

Moths in the Iron Curtain or Roaming in the USSR with Al Purdy and Ralph Gustafson

One may argue that that the Iron Curtain was not lifted, but simply that the West-East moths through decades of nibbling at it from both sides made holes in its fabric, holes so big that the curtain has become almost invisible.

In October of 1976, Al Purdy and Ralph Gustafson were parachuted behind the Iron Curtain under the aegis of an agreement between the Canadian Department of External Affairs and the Kremlin, with the USSR Writers' Union playing the host. Their wives, Eurithe and Betty, introduced to me by Al as 'the female chauvinist chaperones,' and by Ralph as 'the indispensable,' came along and the Writers Union hired me, at the time a post-graduate student of American journalism at the Moscow University School of Journalism, to be their interpreter and travel companion for their twenty-one days of travelling.

Formally, the purpose of this three-week venture was for the first Canadian authors visiting the USSR to make contacts and familiarize them with the country. As Ralph put it, "humanness recovered, prejudice erased, misconceptions dismissed." Accomplished or not, the mission resulted in two books, whose titles alone tell much about the characters of their authors. Al Purdy's *Moths in the Iron Curtain* was first published in 1977 (by Black Rabbit Press in Ohio). Ralph Gustafson's politically correct nineteen Soviet Poems, gracefully filled with his sensitive judgments, was published in 1978. As far as I know, neither was translated into Russian. However, Al's book did attract Moscow's attention even before it was printed. In fact, the Union of Soviet Writers would have loved to stop Al from publishing the book. A few months after Al returned to Canada, I received a call from an official of the Foreign Commission of the Writers' Union.

"Do you and Purdy write to each other?"

We had. We exchanged letters and even smoker's gifts. Al smoked cigars and I a pipe; I sent Al Cuban cigars that were difficult to get in Canada but inexpensive in Moscow during the era when friendship between the two communist states was at its highest, and Al sent me Dutch pipe tobacco, a rare luxury in communist Russia.

"Did he write to you about his new book?"

He had. A few months after the trip, Al sent me a letter with the introduction to his new book of Soviet poems: "I enclose an article,"—he wrote—"which will be published with the small book [of poems]. There may be some things you won't agree with in it, but I'm sure you couldn't say the piece expresses anything but friendly feelings." I liked the article, but obviously some officials in the Union of Soviet Writers didn't. They especially didn't like the title.

"What exactly does he mean by the 'Moths in the Iron Curtain?' Who are those 'moths?' The Soviet people?"

"I don't think he meant that."

"We don't care what he meant, but we do care what he writes about us. And if that was the impression he was left with after his trip, then all of us and especially you are in trouble. Perhaps, at least he'd consider changing the title. If he is your friend, he'll understand."

I couldn't completely follow this 'friendly' advice. My letter to Al was nothing but the usual 'how are you?'; only in the postscript did I casually mention that the title seemed a little odd to the Writers' Union.

Al got the hint right away. Not that he was prepared to change anything (I could hear his familiar "the hell I will . . ."). He didn't care much about his poems being translated into Russian, though he certainly remembered and even briefly mentioned in his introduction the story I told him about my experience with the translation of Arthur Miller's story "Fitter's Night."

In 1969, Miller and his wife Inge Morath, a photographer, spent a few weeks travelling in the USSR. After the trip Miller published *In Russia,* a book that offered his impressions of Soviet society, and highlighted his campaign for the freedom of dissident writers. Soon all Miller's stories and plays, even those that fully met all the requirements of 'socialist realism' were banned in the USSR. Not aware of the ban, I translated his story, 'Fitter's Night,' and offered the translation to one of the national magazines. The editor liked it, but suggested we wait a few months and perhaps as he put it the wind of change from the 'Old Square,' a nickname for the HQ of the Communist Party Central Committee located in the Old Square of Moscow, would bring Arthur Miller back to the Russians.

One night, over the usual nightcaps I told the story to Al. 'If you see Miller, tell the story to him.' Al grinned and after a few more nightcaps added, "I would, but Miller moves in much more cultured literary circles than me."

Years later, after the collapse of the Soviet Union, my translation of 'Fitter's Night' was published in one of the last strongholds of the country's socialist past, *The Socialist Labor Magazine.* But in 1978 when Al and I corresponded about his upcoming book, neither of us could have imagined that fifteen years later the wind of change would grow so strong that on its shoulders I'd relocate to Canada or that in the summer of 1993 Al and I would be laughing over our USSR memories in Ameliasburg sitting on the porch of his Roblin Lake house or that, much to my surprise, Al would be washing down his jokes with herb tea, not vodka.

Anyway, in his reply to my letter Al armed me with the interpretation that was meant to sweeten the pill for the Soviet officials. "Your postscript disturbs me," he wrote, "and apparently I have to explain the title. I suppose 'iron curtain' is a Western term, denoting the difficulty of entering the Soviet Union and that the West thinks the Soviet Union has an inflexible rigidity. Okay...we [Purdy and Gustafson] were moths in the sense that we had no difficulty entering the S.U., and that we chewed up a little of the iron curtain since relations were cordial."

Al's introduction was the only part of the book I read at the time. Thirteen poems written by Al after the trip (as well as Gus' nineteen poems) I read only eighteen years later when my family and I relocated to Canada. I was pleasantly surprised to see that my name was first in the list of those Al dedicated the book to "*With cordial greetings* . . ." Reading the poems brought back memories that seemed almost lost, and Al was right, the poems expressed nothing but friendly feelings, though some episodes we remembered differently.

Pre-impressions and Myths
Back in the USSR, we talked and joked about many things, trying to avoid politics: Al, because he thought that talking about the ways the Soviets conducted their affairs would be in bad taste from a guest, and I, because I realized that both Al and Gus would write about their experiences in the USSR and their conversations with the people they befriended. I had to watch what I said.
In *Moths in the Iron Curtain* Al wrote, "Victor…and officials from the Writers' Union quickly dispelled one pre-impression I had of the Russian character, that it was solemn and rather self-important." On my part the pre-impression I had about the Canadian character, that it was a silent type, was quickly dispelled by Al's openness and sense of humor.
In Moscow, the delegation stayed in the Sovietskaya Hotel, built around the once famous Yar Restaurant. Chekhov and Rasputin had dined there. In the Soviet days, the hotel was reserved for the communist apparatchiks and foreign dignitaries. As Al rightfully noted, "it was slightly old-fashioned, but provided solid bourgeois comfort."

The first night we paid must-do visits to the Red Square, the Kremlin, and St. Basil's Cathedral. Al described it in his book as "of a size not overwhelming, its colors . . . like a child's first discovery of magic in ordinary things." He couldn't believe that "the supposedly dour Russian character have produced those flashing painted towers, so much like Disneyland without the vulgarity." I dared not dispel his bewilderment with the mysterious Russian character. The official history insists that Russian architect Posnik Yakovlev, nicknamed Barma, 'the mumbler,' designed the cathedral and that Ivan the Terrible put out his eyes so that he could never build anything so beautiful again. This may be no more than a myth. Between 1475 and 1510, Italian architects were employed by the Russian tsar to restore the Kremlin. Who knows, perhaps that explained "those flashing painted towers?"

Another Day, Another Myth Dispelled
For the trip to Yasnaya Polyana, Leo Tolstoy's country estate, which had been preserved as a national monument, the Writers' Union booked a Chaika, a big black powerful limousine usually used by high-ranking Communist officials and the military brass. Driven like a rocket by what Al called a "mad Soviet cosmonaut," the limo cut left of our

lane of traffic with cops standing at attention: "They salute you," I pointed to one. "Finally," grinned Al.

The estate museum safeguards the legends of Count Tolstoy's last years when he tried on the roles of a simple plowman, a stove builder, a carpenter, and a boot maker as ways to escape the life of a wealthy count. Despite the murmur of the official guide, the hypocrisy did not escape Al's sharp eyes. In his poem "Visiting Tolstoy," a monologue for voices, he wrote: "Master the plow is ready – Vladimir is holding the horses – and the old bent-backed tiny behemoth of letters pretends he's a character in his novels pretends he's a peasant... Who's he kidding?"

International Incidents

Some episodes that Al called "international incidents" we remembered differently. But there was one that neither Al nor Ralph ever knew about. We landed in Tashkent late at night straight into the waiting arms of the Uzbekistan's Branch of the USSR Writers Union and the 'la fourchette' windy speeches lavishly sprinkled with vodka.

Despite the warning that the hordes of participants to the Afro-Asian writers' conference which was scheduled for that week in the Soviet Uzbekistan would most likely flood the Samarkand hotels, Al and Ralph insisted on going, inspired by a quest to find the muse as great as the one that once possessed the fifteen-century Uzbek poet Alisher Navoi. In fact, it was I who badly needed lots of artistic *inspiration* in order to secure space in what I heard was the only decent Samarkand hotel (Al called it "crummy"). I asked the Writers' Union head office for help, but the "hand of Moscow" failed us.

"Think of something" was all the advice I had. The Intourist office was in a small room on the second floor of the two-story building of the Samarkand Airport. It was September, but the nights were still hot, and the sweat was trickling down the soiled collar of the only rep on duty. "Nyet" was the verdict. Poets, he said, were not on his priority list. In the hall a group of American tourists were sharing the wind from the only fan with the Purdys and the Gustafsons, all-unaware of the ongoing clash. Suddenly, it dawned on me - Sharof Rashidov, a poet too, his portrait on the wall behind the rep's back, was at the time the Communist Party leader in the Uzbek Soviet Socialist Republic and a candidate member of the Politburo.

"These Canadians," I lowered my voice, "are here on his personal invitation." On my mention of Rashidov's name, the rep rose from his chair, bent over the desk and narrowed his eyes at me. For a minute his hand rested in hesitation on the telephone. I did not blink.

"The tall one," I pointed to Al, "may be translating Rashidov's poetry into English." The rep hesitated for another minute, then asked for our passports and scribbled our names onto the hotel voucher. I knew there was neither way, nor will for him to verify my words. Al and Ralph never found out what true lies got us rooms in overcrowded Samarkand, but they were happy; especially Al for getting ahead of the bunch of American tourists. Once at the hotel Al went to bed and I took Eurithe, Betty and Ralph to look at the turquoise domes of Samarkand mausoleums by moonlight.

Early next morning, after the muezzins called the remaining faithful to prayer, Al wanted to see the local marketplace. It was Sunday and we walked the narrow time-battered streets passing donkey carts filled with local produce to what was then Kolhozniy Rynok, the collective farmers' market. The day was getting hot. Al treated himself to a tongue-burning shish kebab and wanted to cool it down with a piece of freshly cut watermelon. Nearby, a farmer in black sateen *tubeteika*, an Uzbek skullcap, and pale blue cotton gown tightly tied with a colorful waistband was slicing watermelons with a knife. Al took a piece, but then he saw the farmer's little girl sitting in the shadow of a tree behind the cart, licking ice cream. Al put the watermelon back on the cart, quickly walked to the girl, his camera hanging from his neck, his finger pointing to her face. Communism or no communism, in some lost-in-time Central Asia villages, photographing women's faces was taboo. Of course, all Al wanted was to know where he could buy an ice cream. Before I could interpret Al's silent question, the farmer rushed towards him, bull's anger in his red eyes, a whip in his hand. I grabbed the whip and for a minute or two we stood there looking into each other eyes, me trying to explain something about ice cream, him still suspicious of Al's intentions. A few locals gathered around us and helped me to dispel the man's fears and though reluctant, he let go of the whip.

  Back in the hotel we joined the rest of the team for a quick tour of Samarkand that ended on a laughing note, erasing from memory the sour taste of the morning's "international incident." Valentina, our Intourist guide, was walking us through the ancient capital of Tamurlane's empire to the remains of what was once the biggest mosque in Central Asia—Bibi Khanum Mosque. Amir Timur (Tamurlane) started erecting the mosque around 1399, after his successful campaign to India, but it was not finished before a new campaign required him to leave. His wife, Bibi Khanum finished the construction in his absence. "When Tamerlane returned," summarized Valentina, "he went to see the mosque. In front of his look raised in their magnificence were the domes and minarets. Amazed that he possessed such a wonderful erection, he hurried to his wife."

"I'd drink to that," laughed Al and on this encouraging note we hurried to the airport to return to Tashkent and later take a five-hour flight to yet another ancient city, this time in Eastern Europe.

The scenery changed from the turquoise domes of mausoleums and mosques to the golden domes of Ukrainian churches. For three days in Kiev, the Purdys and the Gustafsons were imbibing culture and beer while touring the ancient monasteries, the Shevchenko Museum and the Conservatory. Craving for fruit in the fruitless Soviet Kiev we passed others with the same craving: "people cluster in queues to buy them" ("Make Watermelons Not Love" - Al Purdy). One hot afternoon Eurithe wanted to stop for a watermelon right under a "no stopping" sign. Guests' wishes, especially those of foreign delegations, always came first in the USSR and the driver stopped. We joined about twenty locals queuing for the melons. Soon a traffic cop appeared and ordered our driver to move. Eurithe and the Gustafsons obediently headed back to the car ready to give up on the watermelons, but not Al. Looking down on the short figure of the cop he showed him his Canadian passport, and then pointed to the watermelons, declaiming something about freedom, Canada and human rights, and the meaning of true democracy.

Meanwhile, the vendor reached from behind the counter and put a watermelon in my arms ending another international incident. Watching Al challenging a traffic cop in Kiev made me believe that somewhere across the ocean there was a land of harmony between motorists and traffic cops. I parted with this illusion many years later when at 2 a.m. I was pulled over for driving fifteen kilometers over the limit on Bayview Avenue in Toronto: reasoning with traffic cops turned out to be a bum show on either side of the ocean or political system.

On our last day in Kiev, before the official meeting and lunch at the Ukrainian Club of the USSR Writers Union, the local guide took us to Babi Yar, a ravine in Kiev, the site of the massacre of Jews by the German Nazis in 1941. About twenty percent of the almost one million people who lived in Kiev before the war were Jews and those who failed to escape the besieged city were shot in Babi Yar. Later, Soviet prisoners of war, Jewish and non-Jewish, and Roma, were also killed there. For political reasons, no official memorial was built at the site until 1976 and even then, it did not even mention that most victims were Jews. Only a few poets and musicians dared to challenge the Soviet propaganda machine. In 1961, during 'Khrushchev's Thaw,' Yevgeny Yevtushenko's powerful poem "Babi Yar" was published and echoed in 1962 by Dmitri Shostakovich's 13th Symphony.

Al and Ralph were crushed by what Al called the "enormous not murder only, but a black cloud in the human brain . . .." The story of a Russian sergeant whose soldiers found babies' shoes even years later when training near the site made us feel hollow and sick inside— "all of us are their descendants," Al wrote in his "At Babiiy Yar."

At the hotel, Mark Pinchevsky, the editor of *Vsesvit*, the Ukrainian journal of world literature, was waiting for group to take us to the formal summing up meeting of the Ukrainian leg of our tour. The Writer's Club was close, and Mark offered to walk with Al and show him some interesting spots on the way. Worried about the "interesting" spots, I tried to talk Al out of it, but his settled policy at the time was "never refuse a drink. Mark assured me that it'd be "just a snifter for an appetite," so we agreed to meet later at the meeting. Little did I know that a snifter would be a tall glass of brandy on an empty stomach? When Mark and Al, both wearing dark glasses, showed up at the meeting it had already descended into the usual "here is to peace" speech-toast smoothed down the irksome guests' throats with black caviar and vodka. The *pretentiousness* of the situation did not go well with Al. "Peace...damn your eyes!" he cursed through gritted teeth: "They'd better leave their dissident writers alone and admit the truth about Babi Yar."

A few days in Riga and Leningrad were very much the same, perhaps, with the exception of one episode in a small, but lavish, Baltic Writer's Council brunch in an elite resort hidden from public eyes behind the pine trees and sandy dunes of Jurmala, near Riga. After a dozen of 'here is to..." the carefully selected group of Latvian writers turned to singing. Suddenly, the communist consciousness cracked and a popular local stage director and repertoire Peteris Peterson broke out off-key with "*Deutschland, Deutschland über alles*" ('Germany, Germany above all'), once a Nazi anthem. Al, who during the war was with the RAF's Military Police, bent over the table and stared down his throat. "I can see his tonsils, but not what he means," he said turning to me. "Whom is he aiming at?" Many years later, having read about the ex-Nazis parading in Latvia,

I no longer wonder.

Back in Moscow, on the eve of the return flight home, Eurithe and Betty were shopping in the hard currency stores reserved for foreigners and the diplomatic community. Al and Ralph were drafting notes for the politically correct speeches required at the summing up meeting with the Soviet officials, were eager to hear appreciation of the Soviet way of life in the "Communist paradise." It was decided that Ralph would do the talking.

At the end of the meeting Al added that Soviet tradition impressed him—the way the Soviets honored their writers and academics. The cities we visited had squares and streets named after the most prominent ones. "I cannot think of a Canadian parallel," he said.

Al and I corresponded for a few years. We met again only seventeen years later, after me, my wife Natasha, and our thirteen-year-old son relocated to Canada. One day, we read in a newspaper about Al Purdy's readings in Toronto's High Park. Eurithe was with him.

We waited behind the improvised park stage. That evening in the coffee shop at the York Hotel we laughed and talked about his USSR adventure and our future in Canada.

"How about a snifter to that?" said Al, "Only now," he added looking at Eurithe, "I toast with herb tea, damn it."

Works cited:
Purdy. Al. *Moths in the Iron Curtain*. Illus. Eurithe Purdy. Sutton West: Paget, 1979. Print.

***

VICTOR POGOSTIN

Virgin Lands - Sputniks and Painless Parker

(The Virgin Lands campaign was Nikita Khrushchev's idea to boost the Soviet agriculture. Starting from the late 1950's, early 60's Student Construction Teams were sent to build agricultural structures primarily in Kazakhstan.)

On Fridays, our weekly bath days, we were driven fifty kilometers to a local administrative center Balkashino that had a hot bathhouse. It was dark when we were coming back. Unexpectedly our truck began to slowly slide into the roadside ditch. We quickly jumped over the side on to the firm grassy ground. We were stuck in the wilderness of the black steppe with only bleak light coming from the low, scarcely starry sky. Suddenly the sky lit up as if a giant floodlight flashed directly above our heads. A powerful ray of light hit the steppe snatching it from the darkness of the night. Gradually the floodlight moved up and then after another flash dissolved in the sky. Next morning, we heard on the radio that Sputnik "Voshod" was launched on August the 28, 1964.

    The village of Doroginka where we were building two rubble sheepfolds was twenty-five hundred kilometers away from Moscow and over a hundred kilometers away from the Kazakh town of Atbasar. The village had four streets. A narrow rivulet divided it into the Russian, German and Kazakh sections. Some of the local Germans were the descendants of the russified Volga German settlers brought here by Katharine the Great others were children and grandchildren of the technical specialists invited by Stalin in the late 1920s, early 30s to help with the country industrialization and deported to Kazakhstan and Siberia after the outbreak of World War II. Those were the lucky ones. Large numbers of the German community in Russia ended up in labor camps or simply disappeared.

A shabby log building of an old school whose classrooms were converted to bedrooms for our Student Construction Team stood on the outskirts of the village.

On the Kazakh side there were low clay houses with thatched roofs and adjoining mud-brick structures for livestock. Beyond the village stretched out the yellow-greenish steppe intersected by dusty roads.

Victor Moroz, the team's driver woke me up at dawn. It was my and Vlad Kr—ko turn to go to Krasnaya Polyana sandpit, located twenty kilometers away from our village, next to a quarry.

It rained at night. The roads were muddy, and in order not to bog down in the mud he drove on grass tailgating the leading truck. This was not the first time I have traveled with him, and I remembered how he complained that the brake pads were worn out and he had to slow down gradually switching the gears first to neutral and then gradually to low speeds.

"Vic," I said. "Why are you dogging him? What if he stops suddenly and you have no brakes?"

"Don't fret." Vic grinned. "He has no brakes either."

The sand was wet from rain and heavy to load and it took us an hour to fill up the back of the truck and level the sand so that it would not press on the sides. Vic turned the ignition on, but the engine coughed and stalled.

"What now?" I asked.

"Fucking gas pump stuck. Too hot...should be OK in half an hour."

The sun was already baking hot. Not far from the sandpit was a river that looked very inviting, and we walked down the cliff for a dip. The bottom was sandy too, but firm, and the water was clear blue. A pike froze motionless near the shore, but as soon as our shadows fell on the surface of the water, it darted to the side and disappeared.

The quarry was across the river. Convicts from one of the nearby prison camps were brought there to mine the stone. The convicts wore gray caps, gray jackets and moved leisurely. The bored guards kept an eye on them from a distance sitting by the field kitchen, ready for lunch. Occasionally, we too would come to this quarry to get rubble for our sheepfolds.

Hot days, cold nights, lack of any produce and millet porridge for breakfast, lunch and dinner had taken a toll on many of us. I escaped the cold but had a severe toothache. The nearest clinic that had a dentist was two hundred kilometers away at some no-name railway junction. The driver of a truck sent there to pick up cement for our construction site agreed to give me a lift. For nearly five hours I jolted on bumpy roads in the open truck. It was dark when I came to the clinic. The dentist's office was at the end of a long corridor, separated from the clinic's ambulatory by a plywood partition. It was Saturday and the dentist, a truly russified German, had already had one or two glasses of pure medical spirit. Never mind my aching tooth, he could hardly find my mouth. A sturdy red-haired nurse watched his manipulations with curiosity. Finally, he gave up and asked me to wait in the corridor.

Sitting there I could hear him instructing the nurse how to pull out my tooth. I learned that my head pressed tight to her bosom and her left hand should hold my jaw.

"Then put your right arm in a lever position,

grab the tooth and pull and all will be square," he said.

Soon I was called in. The dentist shook my hand and walked unsteadily out the door.

The redhead cheerfully informed me that I was her first patient, and she would do her best and I wouldn't feel a thing.

"Open your mouth, sweetie," she said and showed me a large plastic syringe bulging with solution. "We use it for large cattle," she chuckled.

Indeed in a few minutes I could neither feel my mouth nor even speak. Inspired by her success the redhead remembered that dentists usually talk to their patients.

"What's your name Blue-eyes?" she asked.

"Viiic," I mumbled.

Pulling no further punches, she, like a true fighter, grabbed my head with her left hand, pulled it close to her huge bosom so that I could hardly breathe. With her right hand she pushed the forceps in my mouth and with a crack produced half of my tooth.

"Well," she said puzzled. "Guess we'll need a hammer and a chisel to get the other half."

Thank God not a hammer and sickle, I thought looking at a large poster pinned to the wall featuring a woman-collective farmer happily clutching a sheaf of wheat and a sickle to her chest.

In about an hour the other half of my tooth was pulled out. I still felt nothing, nor did I know what her chisel had done to my gum.

"Drink it when the freezing is off," said the redhead and gave me half a bottle of vodka. "You've earned it."

I staggered to an abandoned logwood house converted to drivers' hostel. My driver was there tipsy and relaxed. He listened to my story with sympathy, drank my vodka and said: "Listen..., you won't sleep anyway. Keep an eye on the truck..."

His loaded-with-cement truck was parked in the nearby wasteland. The night was cold. A huge red moon hung low over the wasteland. Somewhere in the darkness of the steppe the wolves howled, and I piteously echoed them.

***

Putsch

They were turbulent days in October 1993. A power struggle between President Yeltsin and the Russian Parliament was imminently leading to an armed standoff and the premonition of civil war hung in the air.

On October 3, 1993, my friend Michael N-k suggested we meet for lunch. A PhD in philosophy Michael started his own philosophically undefined business and wanted to see if there was an opportunity to go international. "It is Sukkot too," he said. "We can talk business and celebrate."

Sukkot or no Sukkot, the Moscow restaurants of the 90s offered a fit for all nonreligious menus. Only a few weeks ago a kosher member of the American Sociological Association called me in the morning from the Hotel Budapest. He believed his waiter could not understand him. He ordered kosher yogurt and lox and bagel, and the waiter brought slices of ham and sour cream. I got the waiter on the phone and after listening patiently to my explanation, the waiter said, "Tell him that I understood him. He is free to order whatever he wants, and I bring what we have."

The restaurant on the second floor of the "Moskva" Hotel was no exception and we were happy to indulge in Olivier salad, assorted ham and pork chops and as a kosher supplement a bottle of Stolichnaya.

At about 5 pm we were enjoying our get-together when the neighboring guests rose to leave and crystal chandeliers started flashing signaling closing time. Our waiter came looking a bit nervous.

"Mind paying now?" he asked. "We are wrapping up."

"Isn't it a little early?" I replied.

"There's something, like, going on over there." He motioned to us to turn around and look at the Manezhnaya Square and the Kremlin.

The square was deserted, no cars, no passers by.

We finished our meal and walked down to the hotel lobby right in the midst of soldiers in full combat gear - helmets, raincoats, machine guns with bayonets attached. A colonel came up to us.

"You better hurry home," he said.

"What's happening?" I asked.

"Putsch," he said matter-of-factly. "The Kremlin may be stormed."

"Why're you here?"

"Just in case... We don't have our orders yet."

We walked round the corner to the Revolution Square.

Across the square the few people walked quickly towards the arched subway entrance. Only two lonely cars, Michael's and mine, remained parked in the usually crowded parking area in the back of the hotel.

Two soldiers and a traffic policeman stood nearby. We thought he was waiting to see who'd come from the restaurant and first hesitated to get behind the wheel, but the policeman urged us to leave.

I circled a small park with a huge grey stone monument to Karl Marx, passed the Bolshoi Theatre and at the corner of Maneshnaya Square turned right onto deserted Tverskaya Street towards Leningradsky Prospect. Somewhere in the area of the Belorusskaya railway station, my Lada was overtaken by two open trucks full of men in camouflage jackets shouting loudly and waving machine guns. The trucks turned onto Sheremet'yevskaya Street heading to Ostankino TV Centre.

The evening news broadcasted messages and images about riots in Moscow; breaking of police cordons around the Parliament building; calls by the rebellious members of Parliament to seize the Mayor's Office and attempts by the armed groups led by General Makashov to storm Ostankino TV Centre.

Late that night, PM Yegor Gaidar went on TV and addressed the Muscovites urging everyone who cared about democratic gains to gather near the Moscow City Hall.

With my wife and son in Canada, there was no one to stop me and I went. I left my car near the intersection of Stoleshnikov Lane and Petrovka St. and walked up past the monument dedicated to the founder of Moscow, Prince Yuri Dolgorukiy, towards the red brick walls and high, white-trimmed windows of the Moscow City Hall.

At first glance, there were about two hundred people gathered.

A few babushkas mingled in the crowd, offering tea from thermoses and pies with cabbage and potatoes. The soldiers we had seen in the early evening were nowhere to be seen. For some reason the army was in no hurry to show its support.

Around midnight, a man came out and asked in a megaphone whether there were men with military service experience. Several men, including me, stepped forward. Those who had gathered were divided into groups. My group of about twenty was to take position by one of the Kremlin gates. Soon we were given weapons: long wooden sticks with a looped rubber retention cord. That was it. My impulse to be a champion of democracy dried out. I remembered the trucks full of tipsy fighters with automatic weapons and advised my "warriors" to finish their tea and pies and go home. The group melted away in a matter of minutes. I walked back to my car leaving the defense of democracy to the natural course of history.

On October 4, the rebellious Congress of People's Deputies and the Supreme Soviet were dispersed by President Yeltsin, the troops that had finally reached Moscow stormed the White House and the leaders of the resistance were arrested.

***

Part Two - At A Far Meridian

In the fifth year at the Faculty of Translation, the time came for the internship abroad. It was part of the educational process and in late December 1966 I left for India to work for the Soviet Trade Mission energy group and returned from my internship in March of 1968.

Bon Voyage

After the final interview in the Central Committee of the Communist Party of the Soviet Union my travel documents were finalized and my departure for probation in India was scheduled for early December 1966.
"I'll call you in about a week and your ticket and passport will be ready." A woman-referent in The Ministry Of Energy Section on Foreign Relations smiled and wished me "Bon Voyage."
I waited for a few weeks, but no one called. The referent was stunned when I called her.

"Where are you?" she asked.
"Home, in Moscow."
"Please hold."
I heard her ruffling through papers and then she whispered.
"Come soonest," she said, "I'll meet you at the back entrance to the Ministry and don't forget your internal passport."
"My fault, I thought you had already left," she said when we met.
She exchanged my internal passport for the "foreign" passport issued only to those who travelled abroad, gave me an Air ticket payment order for Aeroflot and urged me to get on the first available flight to Delhi.

A heavy blizzard blew a thick snow blanket over the narrow side road to the Sheremetyevo Airport. Our driver missed a barely visible road sign, and I barely missed my flight. Luckily it was delayed and in late December 1966, I landed in Delhi.

On arrival there was a commotion at the airport as the Soviet Embassy officials were fussing over a well-dressed woman shepherding her to a waiting limousine.

In the Embassy the security officer examined my papers, checked something in his log and gave me an inquisitive look.

"Where were you past two weeks?"

"In Moscow. Why?"

"You were scheduled to arrive two weeks ago."

"Well," I said attempting to make a friendly joke. "I stepped out for a walk in the Himalayas."

It was a non-stop flight and I noticed that my sarcasm was ill-received.

I tried to right the wrong and told him about the confusion at the Ministry.

"And today," I added. "I was late again because there was a woman at the airport causing delays."

His look changed from inquisitive to dirty.

"I advise you to forget what you saw today," he said. "And don't forget to register with our 'Fizkulturnaya' *(Athletes)* for the Komsomol organization." Along with Profsouznaya (*Trade Union*) for the Communist Party organization – these were euphemisms used by the Soviet propaganda abroad to camouflage the Soviet ideological institution's blunt role in controlling the work and life of the USSR Embassies and Trade Missions.

Many years later, watching a TV series about Svetlana Alliluyeva, Stalin's daughter, I realized that we had been on the same flight to Delhi, and she was the woman that caused commotion at the airport. It was in India that Stalin's daughter defected to the West in April of 1967.

***

Kasimpur

I was assigned as a translator to a colony of Soviet specialists building the Harduangj Thermal Power Station in the village of Kasimpur located north of the city of Aligarh in the state of Uttar Pradesh.

The village stretched along the bushy shores of a canal connecting the Ganges and the Jumna Rivers. The locks on the western edge of the village created rapid waters and the locals fished for phazans near the locks.

At night, when it cooled down, I used to walk in the wild mangroves along the canal and watch river snakes making long winding paths when they slid from high grass into murky water.

The Soviet specialists lived close to the construction site. The lucky ones shared semi-detached cottages built for Indian engineers who would come later to operate the Power Station. The majority though lived in shed houses. After a few weeks of sharing a cottage with two engineers I moved into one of the bachelor apartments in the long row of sheds. My only company was a family of rats that lived in its cramped attic. Every day I checked the metal screens in the kitchen and bathroom drains and the ceiling plywood for holes. The rats raced loudly all night but after a while I got used to their scratchy feet-beat and slept well. In two months, I relocated to a small brick and concrete room adjacent to our club. There too I had a tenant: a large green-headed snake lived under my porch.

We coexisted peacefully – I never attempted to evict the snake and the grateful snake took care of all approaching rodents.

The only window in my room was blocked by an old and noisy air conditioner. On hot nights, if it failed, I slept wrapped in a soaked in cold waterbed sheet. The sheet dried up quickly and had to be re-soaked every two hours.

One day I asked our host Superintendent why did we have to endure such discomforts? He smiled and offered me a short ride to Aligarh. There in a well-groomed residential area he showed me a spacious beautiful house surrounded by a lavish garden with a sparkling clear blue swimming pool.

"Look…," he said. "We leased this house for you folks, but your Chief refused to move in. It sits empty and costs us a fortune."

Next day I asked the Chief "Why?"

"Up there…" He raised his finger. "I've been advised not to go for a house in the city. God knows where you rascals would have ventured at night. Who'd watch you? Better here… nowhere to go and my ass is safe."

***

Communist maxims put to test

Our train arrived at the Allahabad Junction at dawn. The cooling night breeze from the nearby 'Triveni', the meeting point of India's two largest rivers, the Yamuna and the Ganges, and the underground Saraswathi rivulet had died, and the town plunged into the sweltering late May heat. Nothing, not even air stirred in the sunlit railway station square. It was Friday, a sacred day for Muslims and most of the city businesses and shops were closed. There were no cabs. The Station Master explained that the town cabs, all five of them, were busy serving a large wedding.

The only transport available was a flock of cycle rickshaws hiding from the sun in the shade of the station arcade.

They immediately spotted us and pedaled over, offering their shiny smiles and lifesaving cart tops. "We don't ride rickshaws. We are not like some fucking imperialists who exploit human beings," said my Chief.

Indispensable as they were in India, the rickshaws were a taboo for the Soviets. One of the main communist maxims forbade any exploitation of one human being by another.

"Sure," I said. "But it's their only way to make a living."

"It is their problem," he said. "And our way, is the only true one."

Our hotel was about two miles away from the station and we started walking there, stubbornly kicking up yellow dust. A few puzzled rickshaws followed. Soon the Chief paused and sat on his suitcase panting heavily. The ideology gave a little *crack*.

"At least let them take our luggage," I said.

"Ok," he agreed reluctantly. "But not a word of this to anyone."

"Swear to God!" I said widening the crack a bit more.

Soaking in sweat we walked on followed by two happy rickshaws proudly carrying our luggage in their carts.

After a swim in the pool, we went down to the hotel restaurant.

A waiter wearing a felt fez with a tassel, a long white cotton shirt and a wide red belt round his waist showed us to a corner table.

"Sahibs are from Russia?" he smiled. "We have Russian salad."

"What's in it?" asked the Chief.

"Pickles, green peas, carrots and chopped pineapple."

"Pineapple? Seriously?" laughed the Chief. "Okay... but Russian salad comes with vodka."

"We don't serve alcohol on Friday. Also, it is

not a vodka place."

"No?" The Chief looked puzzled for a moment. "Whiskey, then."

"I can't," the waiter said, apologetically.

"Call the owner."

A short fat man also wearing a fez came over.

"I can't serve alcohol on Fridays, not in the restaurant."

The Chief, now visibly agitated, wiped the sweat off his shaved head and gave the proprietor his best withering look.

"I can send the drinks to your room." The proprietor tried to compromise.

"We just checked out. We leave tonight," I said.

"It can't be God's will to let us die of thirst," insisted the Chief. "No one will know. We'll engulf the evidence and pay double price."

The last argument worked. We settled for a beer and a small whiskey bottle to go.

To protect the feelings of the other guests, the beer bottles were hidden under the table and our waiter knelt each time he filled the glasses.

It was dark outside when we walked back to the station. The heat-breaking breeze from the Triveni was slowly gaining strength, and happy rickshaws pedaled slowly behind us with our luggage.

Our train was late, and we settled for a long wait in the first-class passengers' lounge. A ceiling

RUSSIAN ROULETTE

fan buzzed over our heads like a giant dragonfly.

"Want some of the 'evidence'?" asked the Chief.

"To maxims that crack under the power of logic." I took a sip.

***

VICTOR POGOSTIN

Impromptu break in the cold war

"Just look at them!" the 'Athletes' *(Komsomol)* activist pathetically pointed the finger of blame at us. *"Look at their eye-concealing sunglasses, pith helmets and shorts! Add a whip and you won't tell them from colonizers and imperialists. Shame!"*
He turned to the audience and a dozen hands clapped approvingly. My friend, a young engineer and I had to solemnly promise that we would never wear pitch sun protection helmets and heat saving shorts not only to work, but most importantly, on our four-day trip to Khajuraho temples. Mercifully, the activist had no clue what the temples looked like. If only he had, we would have never had a chance to admire the carved in stone apogee of erotic art of the 970 and 1030 AD Hindu Temples.

The 'Athletes' and then the 'Trade Unions' committees deliberated for over an hour to okay or not okay our application for the trip. The permission was finally granted, but we had to have a third and more ideologically mature companion to travel with us. The "Third" looked like a stocky, ex-party apparatchik. He received his instructions behind the closed doors.

We went on our journey feeling excited, like truants who had escaped the omnipresent eye of a

School Warden.

The cheapest route was: five hours by train from Aligarh to Agra, then an overnight train to Mahoba and finally the last 78 kilometers by bus to Khajuraho.

The Agra to Mahoba train was scheduled to depart at midnight. We came to the railway station at 11 pm. The platform and even the passenger lounge were suspiciously vacant. When the platform clock showed midnight, I thought it was time to inquire how late our train would be. A tall grey-haired Station Master greeted us with an apologetic smile.

"I am terribly sorry, but your train has left," he said.

"How come?" I asked. "We were here since eleven and there were no trains."

"You are absolutely right, Sir. It came earlier, at about 10:30 and I couldn't keep it for more than 15 minutes. Also, there were no passengers."

"Seriously?" I said.

"Yes, Sir. I completely understand how upset you are and will make sure you are comfortably seated in the First-class lounge and will personally see that you board the next train. Do you prefer a vegetarian or a non-vegetarian section?"

"Fucking Krauts...," said the third when I broke the news to him. He'd learned German at school and now in a foreign country his every other word was *danke schon* or *kaput*.

The next train to Mahoba was at 3 a.m. and we arrived in Mahoba at noon. The bus to Khajuraho was already packed with the locals. The driver left the engine running under the scorching sun and was enjoying tea and chapatti in the shade of a roadside truck stop.

The only foreigner besides us was a man in his thirties dressed exactly as our Komsomol activist shamed us not to - shorts, a pith helmet and sunglasses.

Like us he boarded the bus last minute and now we were squeezed together in the rear of the bus. He was an employee of the US Peace Corps returning home after his term in Tanzania. His ticket allowed him quite a bit of travel and he had chosen to return home via Japan and India. He was well equipped for the trip - not only his attire was adequate for hot weather, but he also had a portable water bottle with a plastic cup and even a flask with whiskey. He offered us a sip, but the 'Third' shook his head disapprovingly.

"Beware of agents- provocateurs," he said. "How do we know if he isn't a secret agent hired to incite us to some illegal action?"

The first and only stop was in Chhatarpur, halfway to Khajuraho. Ignoring all the sanitary recommendations we eagerly pounded on chilled cloudy water with lemon freshly squeezed by the vendor's hardly ever-washed hand. The Peace Corps guy offered us a sip of whiskey. "For disinfection," he said.

The 'Third' gave him a searching look, sighed, took a healthy sip, nodded approvingly and passed us the flask.

"Well, if only for disinfection," he said.

The last leg of our bus ride to Khajuraho was more fun - we sipped from the agent provocateur's flask toasting to pending encounter with Kamasutra sculptures and our impromptu break in the cold war at a far meridian.

***

Tigers hunt at dawn

Holi festival, a festival of colors in late March lasts four days. Four days the rejoicing crowds spray you with washable paint.

The Chair of the Uttar Pradesh Energy Board suggested we escape the festivities and go *shikar* - big game hunting - in the Jim Corbett National Park (the oldest national park in India - established in 1936 as Hailey National Park to protect the endangered Bengal tiger. It was named after Jim Corbett, a well-known hunter and naturalist.) After a four-hour drive across the flat wetlands and mango groves I dozed off and woke up only when our jeep hit the ups and downs of the hilly roads of the northern jungles.

Still drowsy I was trying to make out why the giant pillars ahead of us were swaying in the moonlight. As we drove closer, I realized that it was a caravan of ten timber elephants walking in the middle of the road back to their forest camps. Our host pulled the jeep over and stopped. The sour-smelling caravan slowly walked by throwing up a cloud of dust. When they passed, we got out to stretch and take a leak. Thick bushes and tall reed grass on both sides of the narrow road ended at the foot of the forest ridge that stretched all the way to the mountains.

RUSSIAN ROULETTE

"Keep your rifles at the ready," said one of our guides.

He was probably making fun of us, but after hearing stories about tigers and leopards attacking travellers in open jeeps, we took his words seriously and kept our guns loaded and handy.

We spent the night in the Inspection House of the Energy Board located north of Bareilly. In the morning, two Sikhs, employees of the Board, offered us to join them in hunting a tigress turned man-eater.

They had a wooden cage with a live calf as bait. The cage top and bottom were made of solid, heavy wood with thick, sharp bamboo poles protruding on the sides.

Tigers hunt at dawn. To lure our man-eating tigress, the bait was to be placed in the middle of a small meadow. A special platform was built high around a mighty jungle tree trunk and at midnight we climbed up a retractable ladder on to the platform.

In the moonlight we could see the cage with the surprisingly calm calf. I even thought that it was not his first walk behind the enemy lines and he either was used to it or was scared stiff. He didn't move, even when a family of elephants walked along the edge of the meadow crushing trees on its way. Soon the moon hid behind the clouds and after a few heavy drops of rain a drizzle began.

We soaked wet in our ambush. The tigress didn't bother to show.

"She has her period," apologized one of the Sikh hunters. "And didn't feel like going out. We'll be back tonight. She is dangerous and might kill again."

We couldn't stay and as the first daylight broke through the mist, we left our hideout. Deep in the forest it was still dark. We drove slowly and stopped only once to let a large snake slide across the wet dirt road.

"It's a good hunting sign," said our guide.

He was right. On the way back to the Inspection House we shot two wild ducks and a hare. The house cook made a true hunter's dinner, and we drank to our hosts, to Jim Corbett and the tigresses in heat.

I tried to persuade our Indian companions to share a drink. It wasn't easy, but much to my shame, I made one of them take a sip of vodka.

"I won't be able to walk," he warned.

"Come on...," I said. "Try. Just once."

He did and apparently, he had told the truth. I had to help him get up the stairs to his room.

Next morning, I felt sick. The cold drizzle took a toll on me, and I coughed, and my nose was running. We didn't bring any drugs with us, and I thought I'd try a traditional Russian recipe – a hefty glass of hard liquor. In about two hours we stopped for lunch in a *Dhaba* - roadside eatery - and were comfortably seated on *charpais* cots made out of wood frames and cotton ropes. My Indian friend offered to help with the menu.

"Nothing special," I said. "A healthy glass of whiskey neat to cure my cold and some vegetables."

My tall glass with whiskey was served with the utmost respect and the owner paused behind my back to watch. Cheap local whiskey had a peculiar, disagreeable smell and sipping it was out of the question. As an excuse to down the entire drink in one breath I boastfully said: "Want to see how we drink in Russia?"

"Yes Sir." My Indian friend and Dhaba owner were all attention.

I exhaled and trying not to smell the whiskey tossed it down in one gulp and looked searchingly at the vegetable plate for a bite to help me get rid of the aftertaste. My Indian friend pointed to a tiny green pepper in the middle of the plate. I took a bite and froze stiff. I thought I'd die. Unable to speak or even breathe I fell flat on the charpai.

The owner put an ice bag on my forehead and waved a towel trying to help me breathe. Finally, I recovered my breath and sat up, tears pouring down my cheeks.

"Why on earth did you offer me that pepper?" I asked my scared Indian friend.

"Sorry Vic," he said apologetically. "I thought if you can drink a glass of whiskey in one gulp that pepper would have been a joke to you."

Well, I thought. *One good turn deserves another.*

***

Appendix

On the 7th of November, the night of the Bolshevik Revolution Day celebration, the tables were set up in our club. After the second drink I felt nauseated and went to my room. As vodka cannot be anything but fresh, I blamed the famed Olivier salad, took a heartburn pill, hopped up on the bed and dozed off.

In the still of the night a heavy knock on my door made me jump in bed. There were two chaukidars and an Indian Superintendent of our Colony. "Sahib," Pleaded the Super, "Please come. Your people are fighting, and we can't break up the fight."

A drunken brawl broke out between the two competing "centers of power" – the supporters of the Chief Engineer and those of the Administrative Chief of the Colony.

The conflict had been brewing for many months and closer to the final stage of the project when fewer specialists were required boiled down to who gets the extension to stay in India and consequently makes more of the highly sought after 'Beriozka Checks,' a special currency paid as coupons to Soviet citizens working abroad. These opened up the opportunity to buy foreign-made goods and even Soviet-made cars that otherwise were not available in the stores.

I quelled the fight by threatening that the Indian Superintendent had called the police. Growling both sides, some with shiners under the eyes, others with bleeding noses, went back to their tables and the celebration went on till the last bottle was killed.

Back in my room I tried to sleep, but discomfort in the right side of my abdomen kept me awake. In the morning I couldn't even look at any food. Our driver Sharma took me to a hospital in Aligarh.

The surgeon palpated my abdomen.

"Appendicitis," he said. "Don't wait, operate."

The door to his office was open and from the corner of my eye I saw a large rat leisurely crossing the corridor ignoring the squatting patients. The Doc saw it too.

"Maybe in Delhi," he said.

My boss didn't share the Doc's sense of urgency. "I can't give you our jeep to go to Delhi," he said. "The front axle is lousy and won't last the drive. Wait till next week when we go to the Embassy for mail."

Only a few days earlier the axle was good enough to drive to the upper Ganga wetlands of Narora to hunt the chinkara (Indian gazelle). He and his buddies used to go there every other Saturday night. I was the only one who had a local driving license and he insisted on me joining them.

I didn't want to risk waiting and went to the President of the Indian contractor company that worked on our project. He readily agreed to help. His VP drove me to the Aligarh railway station in time to catch the evening train to Delhi. At the Station he asked me to wait in a lounge and soon came back with the first-class ticket; even a vegetarian dinner on the train was prepaid.

At about 9 pm my cab dropped me off at the Embassy gates. I was put for the night in a small room with four beds in the Embassy hostel and went out to find the Embassy doctor. The guard on duty suggested I might find him in the apartment of his friend, the Communications Security Officer (CSO).

The Doc and his wife were having a drinking and eating binge in the company of the CSO and his wife. The Doc seemed happy to see me. He invited me to the table and handed me a tall glass.

"Vic," he said. "I heard about your problem but..." He filled my glass with vodka. "Honestly, I know nothing about it. Even if I palpate you..."

"I can do it," giggled one of the women.

"Hush!" said the CSO. He too filled his glass and joined the Doc and me.

"Any pain now?" asked the Doc.

"Not really. Just some discomfort."

"Great! Tomorrow you'll go to Dr. Sen's hospital, and he'll tell us what to do. Now relax and have a good time."

We drank and, rightfully so, I forgot about my discomfort and even enjoyed some Olivier salad. Around midnight when the feast was in full swing, we heard a nock on the door. It was a messenger from the Ambassador. The CSO was summoned to the hotline room for a special communication session with Moscow.

The CSO staggered to his feet and left.

"Will he...?" I asked.

"He will," said the Doc.

Half an hour later the CSO staggered back to the room, collapsed in his chair, raised his glass and said: "All square... the party goes on."

In the morning I went to see Dr. Sen. He examined me and suggested to admit me to the hospital not later than 5 pm and he'd operate tomorrow morning. His assistant informed the Embassy doctor whose presence during the operation was mandatory.

I had a whole day to enjoy my freedom. Two stops were on my list - a good movie and dinner.

'Who's Afraid of Virginia Woolf?' was running in the nearby movie theatre. Before the movie I ordered Turkish coffee in the theatre's coffee shop. Back at home I was used to large coffee cups, but this one came in a tiny one.

I drank it in one gulp.

"Encore?" asked the bartender in French.

"D'accord." I played along.

Again, a tiny cup went in one swallow.

"Encore?" The bartender looked surprised.

"D'accord," I said.

After the fourth 'd'accord' the bell rang. I took my seat and prepared to enjoy the famed drama. Ten minutes into the show, the Turkish coffee began to take its effect. I laughed at every tear shed by Elizabeth Taylor. The folks sitting close were throwing angry glances at me and I desperately tried to hold my laughter.

The movie was longer than I expected, and my dinner had to be skipped. At about 5 pm I reported to the hospital carrying a broad silly smile on my face.

My ward was very spacious with a large, mirrored bathroom, a balcony-terrace and even a room for an accompanying relative.

Pre-surgery dinner came in with an apology that it was too late to offer me a full menu.

That is service! I thought. *Worth having an operation.*

Later in the evening two giggling nurses showed up to shave the surgical field and prepare me for the early morning operation.

The poor girls didn't expect to find a hairy body. Perplexed they looked me over and left without saying a word. A male nurse came in carrying a complete barber's kit. He soaped and shaved me from my nipples to knees. Then nurses returned, disinfected the shaved area with manganese solution, left a copy of the The Times of India and some pills on my bedside table and wished me sweet dreams. I went to the bathroom and for a minute and stood stunned – a shaved poodle looked at me from the large wall mirror.

Back in bed I read The Times of India and fell asleep.

A nurse woke me up at 5 am.

"Time, Sahib."

She noticed my night pills untouched and raised her beautiful eyebrows in surprise.

"Slept well?"

"Sure. Why?"

"Those were soporific in case you were nervous and couldn't sleep."

"Oh..."

She pushed a button by my bed and two male nurses rolled in a stretcher.

A few minutes later I was ushered into the operation room. Dr. Sen gave me a reassuring smile and the nurse passed him a syringe.

"Please stretch out your right arm, relax and try

to think of something pleasant," said Dr. Sen.

The Embassy doctor was nowhere to be seen. Remembering his warning, I looked around searching for agents-provocateurs and secret bugs that could have been implanted in my abdomen.

No sign of the agents. On the balcony, outside the surgery room a lonely, disinterested monkey was searching its tummy for lice.

No, not this one, I thought. *Come what may.*

I stretched out my arm.

The Embassy Doc came to my ward after I woke up from anesthesia.

"Sorry," he said. "I couldn't miss a fitting appointment with my tailor. Please don't tell anyone."

He opened his bag and showed me a bottle of whisky.

"Have a sip to your health?"

"Can I?"

He lifted my blanket and looked at the bandage.

"They've sewn you up. It won't spill."

"I'd rather not."

He took two sips - one for him and one for me.

In two days, I could walk by myself and at nights when my tummy hurt, the nurse sat by my bed, held my hand and read me stories from a magazine. If there was no magazine she talked about shopping. Ever since, the mere mentioning of shopping is like a lullaby to me. One night when her touch felt especially tender, I asked her if she'd go out on a date with me.

"Great idea," she said. "But if they see us together, I'll be fired, and you'll have to take me out for the rest of your life."

I never asked her again.

***

RUSSIAN ROULETTE

Coming home

My fifteen months in India ended even more spectacularly than my arrival. Returning home specs were allowed to bring back some extra luggage at no charge.

Bachelor at the time, I had only one suitcase and the Minister-Counselor of the Embassy asked me if I would take a crate of books for an Indologist who was also a son of one of his high-level friends. The Embassy, of course, would give me a letter to the Customs at Moscow. Control over any kind of books brought to the country was particularly strict. As a return favor, he promised to arrange for a week's stay in a nice Delhi hotel prior to my departure. The temptation to have a whole week to myself and finally be able to explore the wonders of Delhi was too much to resist and I agreed.

The Minister-Counselor made good on both promises. I thoroughly enjoyed my week of freedom despite the 5 am knocks on my door by the hotel's tea boys who refused to "go to hell;" not till they had their *baksheesh*.

I even forgave a cab driver that milked my wallet on the first night of my freedom.

I foolishly left the hotel card in the room and after a night on town couldn't remember its fancy Hindu name. I tried to describe how my hotel looked to a shrewd cabbie.

He listened carefully, smiled and after the two hours of touring the city hotels and a hefty sum on his meter dropped me off at mine.

At Sheremetyevo Airport I was one of the first to disembark the plane and the last to get through the Customs. The Customs officer looked at the Embassy letter like a bull at a red tag and I had to wait two hours while two plain-clothes officers ruffled through each and every book. Finding nothing suspicious, they satisfied their zest for confiscation by taking away two anti-fog headlights I'd bought for my future car. True, though, when the Minister-Counselor's high-level friend came to my home to pick up the books and heard the story, my anti-fog headlights were delivered to my door.

***

Comrade Major

"Here they are comrade Major. I tracked them down and delivered as ordered." A young Warrant Officer ushered Serge and me to a small room next to the Store Director's office. We were queuing up at the register when he asked us to step aside and follow him.

It was one of those sunny, but frosty days on the eve of the International Women's Day celebrated on 8 March.

My fellow student, Serge L., had ten dollars and asked me to go with him to the 'Beriozka' hard-currency-only store. He wanted to buy a Japanese umbrella, a present for his girl friend, but was afraid to go by himself for fear of being detained for illegal possession of hard currency.

Although almost a year passed since my return from India, I still had forty dollars left. I kept them wrapped in the official page long document, a proof of currency possession for $140 USD issued by the Soviet Embassy.

"At last." The Major couldn't hide a happy smile. "The day wasn't wasted. Empty your pockets."

He ruffled our stuff with a pen, picked up the currency permission certificate with my remaining dollars and frowned.

"What the hell is that?" he asked, disappointed.

"Currency possession permission," I said.

"Are you telling me you haven't spent your hundred and forty bucks in almost a year?"

"Yes. Should I have?"

"Now don't get smart with me or we'll go and search your apartment."

"Sure, if you have a warrant." Now I couldn't hide my sarcasm.

"Scoffing at me and I am a KGB Major."

He picked up my student ID card, scribbled something in his notebook and counted my money.

"Forty," he said and wrote the number on the certificate. "We'll see how much you've got left when we catch you next time."

In about a week one of the Dean's Deputies who taught translation in my group asked me to stay after class.

"What have you done? he asked.

"Why?"

"I heard our First Department had a letter about your inappropriate behavior."

Bastard, I thought, remembering the Major. The First Department was in charge of the secrecy and political security of the workplace of every enterprise or institution in the Soviet Union.

"My advice," said the DEPDEAN, "After graduation try to get a job in a different region of Moscow. Files are often lost in transition."

***

Taking a Train in England – An Adventure

A colored serpent of railway cars may look attractive and even invoke the sweetest of childhood memories, but it can be very annoying, if you risk traveling by train across the green fields of England.

My wife and I boarded the train in Yeovil, I with a warm feeling of anticipation of the night of 'cheers' with my niece's family in Basingstoke and a deep affection of the good old England and the hospitable Brits.

I ended up in Brighton hating everything from Adam Smith to the Industrial Revolution. It was a hot Sunday afternoon when, after a week in Faro, Portugal, our plane smooth-landed in Bristol and a friend offered to help find a train station in Yeovil – the starting point of, my niece assured me, the shortest and therefore, presumably, fastest route to Basingstoke.

Over the centuries the town had built several railway stations and, though some had been shut down decades ago, the reality was that very few locals seemed to have noticed. After multiple *"Oh, yes it must be this way... oh no, I beg your pardon, that way...,"* we finally emerged by the tiny old-world charm of a station.

A Dickensian, moustachioed specimen of a Station Master welcomed us to his tiny office. After greeting us in his wonderfully articulate baritone, he kindly advised that now we were in the hands of what was once Her Majesty's best in the world railway service and *"oh, yes indeed"* we could leave our worries behind and comfort ourselves with a cup of the best tea one could possibly find in Yeovil. Tea was offered in a cozy tearoom next door to the office.

We waited for the train right in front of the ticket office and the Dickensian character waived us a friendly goodbye. We boarded the nearest car and fell asleep, drowsy after a long trip on a hot day. Two hours into the journey, my wife touched my hand and pointed to a sign on a passing platform. It had an unfamiliar name of 'Something By-Sea.'

"There is no sea in Basingstoke, is there?" she said, her tone reminiscent of my long-forgotten geography instructor.

"England is an island, dear. Any place here is *by-sea*," said I.

A conductor rushed by, ignoring our feeble effort to stop him with a question, and fellow passengers were of little help either. Finally, our "are we in Basingstoke yet?" attracted the attention of a fellow traveler with a distinct American accent.

"I am afraid you are on the wrong track," he said.

"As if the Americans always know…," sighed my

wife.

Well, *this* American was right. What the stationmaster's deep baritone failed to convey was that we should have watched which car we were boarding. The 'best railway system in the world' is so innovative, that the trains no longer run from station 'A' to station 'B.' Not that they do not start at station 'A' – they do – but at a certain junction the many-hued serpent is sliced into two or sometimes three chains of cars and each makes its own journey. Mind you that, at a minimum, at least two of the destinations have nothing to do with the one on your ticket.

Next station was in Brighton; three hours travel time from Basingstoke. Angry and tired, I called my niece and cancelled 'the night of cheers' with her family. Our 'Air Transat' flight to Toronto was to depart the following morning and the Brighton ticket Master offered us tickets for a 30-minute ride to the Gatwick airport hotel.

"Your train is # 5."

"What car?" I asked, but the window was already closed.

It was almost midnight, and we were about to board the train when a lonely figure of a police officer stopped us.

"Going to Gatwick? Then take the next car. That will get you straight to London."

VICTOR POGOSTIN

I felt too tired to argue about the meaning of the word *straight*, not even with Her Majesty's bobby.

***

Part Three - Business *A La Russ*

In early nineties a friend of mine, Yuri R. was relocating to the States. After many years of working for an American Company in Moscow he earned an intercompany transfer on the condition that he would find a replacement.

Yuri offered the three hundred dollars a month job to me. You may laugh, but in those days it was worth it. The Institute of Sociology where I worked as a Senior Research Fellow seemed to be on its last legs, inflation was rampant, and I accepted the offer.

Sidewalk business

In early and even late 90s the hardships of the sudden transition to 'free market' forced almost everyone in Russia into some kind of trade frenzy. Improvised flea markets sprung in parks, stadiums, near the Subway stations, and simply along the cities' sidewalks. Some sold produce grown on tiny garden plots, others - books, used clothes, toys and all sorts of useless junk. The whole city looked like a giant flea market.

One sunny September day, Phil, a Canadian Partner in the Company and I went for a walk. Approaching the Belorusskaia Subway station we passed a long line of babushkas selling all sorts of bric-a-brac displayed on the overturned wooden bottle crates.

"Why would they sell burned out bulbs? Who'd buy them?" asked Phil.

I took him to the nearby electrical supplies store.

"Do you see any bulbs on the shelves?" I asked.
"No."
"Still can't guess why?"
"No. Enlighten me."
"There is a shortage of bulbs."
"So?"
"If a bulb in your home burns out and you can't buy a replacement, what do you do?
"What?"
"Simple. You buy a burnt-out bulb and then you replace a good bulb in your office, institute or factory with the burnt one."
"Wow! How you get so savvy here?"
"Simple. You get it with your mother's milk."

***

The art of negotiations

Phil planned his three-day trip very carefully. He asked for five meetings in three days with two of them on day one.

The first meeting was with a newly created company that was ready to offer its manufacturing services to the North American market. Their flyer had a photo of the office on a large, decommissioned ship docked next to a cargo barge in the North River Terminal in Moscow. Presumably the pictures substantiated the seriousness of their intentions not only to manufacture but also to ship the product to a cargo seaport via the river canal system.

The negotiation room was set up in one of the upper deck cabins. Three men representatives of the host Company entered the room and sat at the table. The meeting started at 10 am sharp, as scheduled.

"Good sign," said Phil. He strongly believed that true restructuring begins in the manufacturing trenches.

"Our proposals," emphatically noted the senior of the three men, and put an intriguing looking attaché case on the table.

"Let's see them," said Phil, and opened his notebook prepared to take notes.

"You are very entrepreneurial," said the boss, "First let's get to know each other better."

A girl dressed like a barmaid entered the cabin with a bottle of champagne and poured five glasses to the brim.

"To friendship," said the boss.

"To friendship," echoed Phil and took a tiny sip.

"What's wrong with him?" The boss looked at me quizzically.

"Canadian," I said, apologetically.

"A hard case," said the boss and turned to Phil and gave him a look.

"To friendship we drink bottoms up."

Phil drank obediently and pointed to the briefcase.

"Not so fast," said the boss.

The barmaid reappeared with coffee, biscuits and a small brandy decanter. Glasses filled; the boss held his out.

"To Canada," he said, looking Phil straight in the eye.

Phil drank and was about to say something when our host rose from the table and gestured us to follow him.

"Now a little surprise," he spoke.

He led us to a red metal door at the far end of the long and narrow corridor. Inside there was a cozy wooden lined relaxation-room with changing cabins, a wooden table with a samovar and a set of wooden chairs. Another door opened into a shower room with two huge wooden barrels one with hot and another with ice-cold water. One more door opened to the steam room with a hot rock stove. The sacred brief case was placed on the table next to a plate with small red caviar and herring sandwiches and a frost-covered bottle of Stolichnaya.

Before I knew it, we had a few ceremonial toasts, undressed and Phil was happily jumping from the hot- to cold-water barrel and back.

The surprise lasted to late lunch served in the former wardroom. I had to cancel the afternoon meeting.

Phil seemed to have accepted the inevitable and went along with the toasts, jokes and Russian viands.

It was getting dark outside, and it was time to leave but the proposal remained sealed in the briefcase.

"No worries," said the boss, "we'll send it to you shortly just need to finalize a few details and now let's drink a small one for the road."

We drank and left feeling baffled and intrigued. Many years passed and we still are.

***

VICTOR POGOSTIN

The road to hell is paved with good intentions

In August 1992, President Boris Yeltsin signed a decree "On the initiation of the system of privatization vouchers." a document that precipitated the transfer of significant wealth to a relatively small group of the newly rich profiteers, former Soviet state and Communist party functionaries and the so-called "Red Directors" - the heads of factories and plants who encouraged workers to sell their vouchers, often by delaying payment of salaries. Within a few years financial and industrial groups, frequently with criminal backgrounds, became the real owners of private factories, plants, banks, industrial and commercial real estate. The majority of Russians had no idea what to do with their vouchers.

Initially the declared value of one voucher in August of 1992 was 10000 rubles ($61.60). With galloping inflation of 2508,85% many Russians opted to sell "the useless piece of paper" for the price of a bottle of vodka. Others, who thought they were more sophisticated, exchanged their vouchers for shares in investment funds.

GUM, the main department store of Moscow, and probably the whole of Russia, opens onto the Red Square and my privatization saga starts from there.

I can't remember exactly on what light pole I

saw the ad about privatization of GUM, but it struck me like a great opportunity to invest all our family vouchers in its shares.

On a sunny cold December Sunday, I drove towards the store only to find out that all the side streets leading to GUM were blocked. Uniformed and plain-clothes police checked the invites and the invitees IDs. The 'Trading House GUM' turned out to be a Closed Joint Stock Company. Alas, my vouchers were strangers at this celebration of life.

Two months later in early 1993 a friend who was the Editor International News at 'Trud' (Labor) one of the National newspapers, called me.

"Still have your derelict vouchers?" he asked. "How about making a killing on investing?"

"Shoot," I said.

"We have an outreach service by the Moscow Realty Fund just for our staff. Get your ass and vouchers over here and I'll square you away."

A formally dressed official presided alone at a desk set by the podium in the assembly hall of the editorial office.

About a dozen conspiratorial looking men and women patiently waited for their turn to take a visitor chair at his desk. It was very quiet in the room as if all those present were performing some mysterious rite.

"Well," I thought, "money loves silence."

I picked up a flyer:
Dear Muscovites: Moscow commercial real estate value would always go up!

The flyer offered me a unique opportunity to become a co-owner of the best Moscow hotels and commercial real estate, including GUM. That, and the assurances that my privatization vouchers will be exchanged for the Fund's shares with six levels of protection worked. I got in line for the bright future of Russian Capitalism. About half a year later I had a job offer in Canada and relocated to Toronto with my wife and son.

Twelve years passed, and family matters brought me back to Moscow. I had never heard from the Fund. But, I said to myself, try to look on the bright side: Moscow realty value was up, Moscow's new Mayor Luzhkov looked like a million dollars, his wife was now a billionaire. So, I thought, *the Fund had been a real cash cow, at least for some chosen Muscovites.*

The Fund had moved, none of its contact telephones were in service and it took me a lot of effort to find it.

"Hello, I am one of your co-owners," I said into the phone.

"Congrats." A female voice on the other end of the line sounded annoyed.

"It seems you are doing well, and I am

wondering what my dividends are?" I asked and gave my shares' numbers.

"Hold," said the voice.

The trifle amount she gave me was less than the cost of a cab ride to their office.

Once a year I go online to check out the cost of the papers. The information is hard to find but there is plenty of advice from other comrades of misfortune and the one I admire most is 'shove it up your...'

***

Project Lifetime

My flight to Toronto was the next day, and I thought I'd spend it with my university buddies, but just one was available on such short notice. The one who could meet asked me for a favor. His friend, the Rector of a Moscow Technological University, wanted to talk about a "project lifetime" that he planned to develop in Toronto.

"Please come," my friend insisted. "And when it's over, I'll drive you to your old place and tomorrow to the airport."

The meeting started at 9 a.m. For nearly three hours I was bombarded with fantasies of how Canada could benefit if their university opened an affiliate branch in Toronto. My job was simple: to secure the government permissions and licensing documentation. The unequivocal answer to my only question, "Who will teach and in what language?" was, "Us, of course, and in English."

I tried to politely shift the discussion from Russian to English. The pundits went silent. In a minute or two, the Rector came to their rescue: "Well, we won't be starting tomorrow... We'll learn or hire interpreters."

I didn't want to be rude, and so when the clock on the wall struck noon, I promised to make some enquiries on my return to Canada and rose to shake hands and leave.

"My friend, why rush?" The Rector would not let go of my hand. "Now we'll move to the most interesting part."

I was escorted to a cozy, wood-paneled room in the basement. The table was already laid with Russian snacks and drinks.

After a few toasts, the Rector was completely relaxed. He took a gun from his back pocket and asked his assistant to put it in the safe. "We are among friends here," he laughed and, reading the question in my eyes, added, "No worries, I have a license. New life. New hot-tempered students from the South, you know."

After an hour, I was determined to leave and, leaving the table for a restroom seemed like a valid excuse. The Rector called one of the charming young girls who served us, and I followed her hip-swaying body to the restroom. It was all white marble with shining brass faucets. The rumors were true; I thought after all, life in Moscow was getting better.

Feeling happier after relieving myself, I pulled the shiny brass handle on the side of the new Italian toilet. Nothing flushed. I tried harder, yet again not a drop of water. Bewildered, I searched the beautiful room for a solution. After a few moments, my charming guide knocked on the door.

"Sir," she called out, "Let me explain."

"Be so kind."

"The construction workers forgot to install the water pipes in the wall. You should look for a bucket in the shower stall."

I opened the shower door and fished out an old, beat-up bucket and a piece of black rubber hose.

"What next?"

"Can you see a small water tap to the right of the toilet? Fill the bucket and flush."

Having broken free from the Rector's party – now in full swing – I returned to my friend.

"Apologies," he said. "He insisted and my son is a freshman there."

***

Part Four -
The Bare Necessities

Among many sociological interpretations of the bare necessities of life I find the Merriam Webster Dictionary definition most simple and straightforward: "...a thing that a person must have in order to survive".

Almost a hundred years ago the mass famine caused by the Civil War in Russia made Lenin, the Chairman of the Council of People's Commissars, to issue a decree that provided senior government and party officials with "medical nutrition rations". Over the following decades the secretly legalized system of special rights, health care, food rations, special clothes stores, housing and other fringe privileges otherwise inaccessible to the citizens of the country grew to enormous proportions creating a barrier between the *nomenklatura* - a select class of people from which appointees for top-level government and Party positions were drawn - and the rest of the population.

My first encounter with the system happened in my student years. I dated a girl that I had met during my winter break stay in the ski recreation center near Moscow.

While my friends and I stayed in the rooms for four or six, she had a private room with bathrooms in a separate building with a 24-hour uniformed concierge on duty. At the time I didn't care to know why.

In May she invited me for a long weekend party at her parents' flat on Kutuzovsky Prospect.

"My folks will be at the dacha, and I'll have girls from our circle," she said. "Invite your friends from your all boys Faculty. The girls feel lonely."

Again, I overlooked her words about 'our circle.'

The morning after the party the long doorbell chimes awakened us. I opened the door. A sturdy man in blue overalls carried a large heavy basket in the hallway.

"Your food orders," said the man.

"Wait, I'll call the flat's owner to pay," I said.

"Who are you?" Asked the man and looked at me inquisitively.

"A friend," I said.

"Just sign for delivery," said the man and left.
"Tania," I called out. "Your food order is here."
"It is a Holiday ration. Open it."
The basket was covered with thick brown paper.

In it there were glass jars with black and red caviar, smoked sturgeon, smoked beef tongue, exotic fruit, fresh vegetables and berries, Finnish salami, even farm eggs, whole chicken, packaged meat, freshly baked pies and a bottle of French Cognac. What surprised me was not only the food that I have never ever seen in the stores, but its quantity. The basket had at least a month's supply of food for a family of four.

"Put the cognac on my dad's desk in his study and the food in the kitchen," said Tania.

"Where do you guys get all this stuff and free?" I asked.

"It is from my dad's work," she said. "We get free food rations on Holidays."

"Where is that great place of work?"

"The Central Committee." She smiled. "Don't tell me you didn't know."

Well, I didn't at the time, but it certainly got me thinking about the dual standards in the social system. Over the years we all had to learn how to navigate through it.

***

VICTOR POGOSTIN

Plumbers come twice

US President Ronald Reagan liked telling a joke about buying a car in the Soviet Union: "A guy in a Soviet country is told he has a 10-year wait for a car. This man laid down the money, and the fellow in charge said to him: come back in 10 years and get your car. The man answered: Morning or afternoon? And the fellow behind the counter said: Ten years from now, what difference does it make? And the man said: Well, the plumber is coming in the morning."

    Our kitchen radiator leaked at midnight. The house maintenance office was closed, and I called the Moscow Central District Emergency Plumbing Service. Surprisingly my call was answered. At about two in the morning, a big, dented truck clanging with pipe trimmings in its back rolled into our yards. Three men in greasy vatniks – Russian cotton and wool padded jackets – got out. They unloaded a rusty toolbox and went up to our doorway. A strong smell of alcohol on their breath was a sure sign that it wasn't their first service call.
    "Who is the boss?" I asked.
    "I am," proudly said the tallest of the three.
    "Come in," I said. "You two wait outside."
    "Where?" asked the boss matter-of-factly and staggered into the kitchen.

He tried to tighten up the leaking tap, but the leak only widened.

"Know what?" he said. "It's as easy as damn it but we won't do it."

"Why?" I asked.

"It won't be fair to you," he said.

"Are you kidding me?"

"Look," he said, philosophically, "this is a two hundred grams of vodka job but there are three of us and we charge a bottle each."

"Well," I said, "I have two bottles and will give you money for the third."

"No," he insisted. "It won't be fair to you. Know what…? We'll shut off the water supply pipe in the basement and tomorrow your house plumber will fix it for two hundred grams, easy-peasy."

"So, twelve apartments will be without water?" I tried to reason.

"No biggie," he said.

They shut the water tap in the basement and left.

In the morning, after a few angry neighbours knocked on my door I rushed to our House Management. Our house was built before the War for the staff of the Air Force Engineering Academy and ever since had been administered by the Main Department of Housing and Communal Services of the Ministry of Defense.

"We don't have new radiators," said the Manager.

"But it is leaking." I tried to reason.

"Exceptions are only for the Heroes of the Soviet Union and disabled veterans of the Great Patriotic War. "

"What about the rest who were born after the War?"

"The rest should get in line and wait."

I waited outside and, in an hour, got hold of our plumber returning from his first morning call. The night crew job estimate was very accurate. Thirty minutes later my leaking radiator had a new gasket. No money was accepted, and the 200 grams of vodka honorarium was consumed on the spot at one gulp.

***

"A car is not a luxury, but a means of transportation"

It took over sixty years for this catchphrase first used in *The Golden Calf*, a satirical novel by Ilia Ilf and Yevgeny Petrov published in 1931 to be translated into Russian reality.

Until then there were four ways to buy a car:

If you were lucky to be tipped off about the occasionally announced registrations of new car buyers at the local Traffic Police Office. People would line up overnight for the opportunity to submit a registered post card with a request for a car. As only those who did not have a car could apply the whole family would show up, stay overnight, and do roll calls to keep their place in line. The line numbers were scribbled in ink on the palms of their hands.

You could get in the long-term line at your place of work and wait for years. Only one or two cars a year had been distributed to organizations and the Communist Party and Trade Union activists were always first in line.

If you were privileged to have an opportunity to work abroad and pay for your car with the special 'certificates,' a special currency paid to

Soviet citizens working abroad. Prices and wait time dependent on the quality of your 'certificates.' For instance, those who worked in the West could convert their dollars, pounds, francs or marks to the highest quality 'no strip certificates.' Next in the hierarchy were those who worked in the Third World countries and were paid with 'yellow strip certificates,' – Beriozka coupons. Lastly, there were the privileged of the lowest grade that worked in the Socialist countries and were paid with 'blue strip certificates.' Finally, once in a blue moon you could win a car in a lottery.

"Pull that dame down...," screeched a woman in a *vatnik* and felt boots with galoshes. That cold December morning a crowd of several hundred Muscovites eager to sign up for a car gathered in a waste lot behind the District Traffic Police station. Most of them were there since evening.

The *Dame* in question was my wife who defied the angry crowd by refusing to put on a vatnik and now stood by the cherished door on the second-floor balustrade of the station dressed in her fashionable swinging sheepskin coat.

My neighbor, a traffic police major, had tipped me off about the planned registration and we came late in the morning. He protected my wife on her way down the 'scaffold.' When she was in the safety of my car, he laughed and whispered: "Not to worry. I just heard the registration was cancelled. Leave before the crowd gets the news."

***

VICTOR POGOSTIN

Black 'Volga' an emblem of authority

I paid for my first and at the time the best Russian car 'Volga' with the 'yellow strip certificates,' hard currency coupons that I earned working in India. Volga was a large, car practically not available in the market, a status symbol.

The post card notifying me of the day I could get a car came in November, nine months after I had paid for it. Two of my closest friends volunteered to help me choose my 'horse.' One of them, a more mature negotiator, brought a bottle of brandy. Early Monday morning we knocked on the window of the 'Beriozka' parking gatehouse, which also required special coupons.

A grumpy attendant gave us a *what the fuck* look that lit up when he saw the bottle. The gates swung open for us forty minutes before the store office opened.

The attendant walked us along the rows of green, grey and white cars to the only black Volga hidden at the far end of the lot. I always wanted a white car, but the inner voice whispered, *Why is there only one black?*

Black Volga was an Executive car of choice for the Soviet nomenklatura.

"Grab it," said the impatient attendant. "Cops would think twice before pulling you over."

My buddies nodded approvingly, vanity got the better of me and the brandy bottle changed hands.

When we came back from the store office with a check stamped 'paid,' we were met by a disappointed Air Force lieutenant general.

"Fellas," he said. "Don't do it to me. I've been looking at this car from behind the fence all Sunday."

"Everyday is not Sunday," philosophically noted the attendant. He filled the car radiator with hot water, started the engine and we drove off.

***

Funny and Poignant

The first long road trip was to the Baltics. My elder brother and one of my best friends went along. The black Volga opened doors to roadside hotels that "welcomed" other travellers with "No Vacancy" signs.

In Estonia we stayed in a camping cabin on a sandy shore of the Baltic Sea. At night we drove to the city downtown looking for a place to have dinner. It was already late, and all cafeterias were closed. Only a night bar was open. Like all night bars in the Soviet days it catered to foreigners, celebrities and high-ranking apparatchiks. We parked in a dark side street and walked to a steep narrow stairway leading up to the welcome neon sign. A heavy built doorman bursting with a sense of power looked down at us and roared in a commanding voice "we are fully booked."

We went back to our black Volga, drove round the corner and stopped right at the stairway. I rolled down my window and called out to the doorman. The behemoth of a man rapidly came down.

"Comrades want a table?" he asked politely.

"For three," I said. "Where can we park?"

"Just round the corner. I'll have the table ready."

***

The rogues and the villains

One night was particularly eventful.

In the spring of 1969, I was on a trainee journalist program at TASS (Telegraph Agency of the Soviet Union). I usually would come there in the afternoon and work late. One of my friends from the Institute days worked there too and occasionally I offered him a lift home. Every so often we'd stop for a late dinner at "Metelitsa" (Blizzard) café on *Noviy Arbat*, a popular neighborhood in Moscow with lots of restaurants and shops. That night leaving the café I saw a man behind the wheel in my Volga. He was messing with the ignition wiring. I told my friend to stay close to the curb and get in the car fast as soon as I push the passenger door open. Then I walked around the car to the driver's side and knocked on the window as if asking for a lift. The man shook his head negatively.

"How about a cigarette?" I asked pointing to a pack on the dashboard.

The man took a cigarette from the pack and rolled down the window wide enough for me to quickly force in my hand, open the door from inside, shove him further in and open the passenger door. My friend thrust in, and we grabbed the man's arms. A few nosy passers-by stopped to watch.

"There is a policeman in the café. Call him," I

asked one of the onlookers.

The policeman and my friend put the man in the back seat and sat on both sides holding him tight. We drove to the nearest police station. Once inside I could see he was slightly built and had a stubbled, expressionless face.

"Straight from the Joint?" asked the officer on duty.

The man sat staring at the floor and said nothing.

The officer looked at his papers, checked something in the log and said, "Hey buddy, you are wanted."

We gave the officer our contact phone numbers and left.

The night was almost over, but not for us. Driving past 'Valdai,' another popular Noviy Arbat restaurant, we saw two men trying to snatch a handbag from a woman. She didn't scream and just stood with the bag clutched in her arms, her back pressed against the construction fence.

I backed up and headed in their direction. The black *Volga* effect worked. The men fled.

"Guys, please drive me home. It is very close," pleaded the woman.

Indeed, her apartment building was nearby in a cozy Arbat lane.

"You don't even know what you've done for

me," she said when we drove to her doorway. "I owe you one. How about dinner at the Berlin tomorrow?"

The invitation was hard to refuse. The Berlin Hotel, originally the Savoy, was in an old Empire style building located in the narrow Rozhdestvenka Street sloping from the KGB HQ on Lubyanka to Neglinnaya Street. In the '70s it was one of the most expensive and hard to get into restaurants, popular with the Soviet elite. Next day we drove to the restaurant and asked the doorman where to park.

A smiling giant in gold-rimmed black jacket and side strapped trousers checked my license plate in his notes and said, "Your friends are waiting for you. Leave the car here. I'll keep an eye on it."

We followed the headwaiter to a private room across the rococo styled hall with a live carp fountain in the center.

The carps could be fished out with a skimmer and cooked for the reveling guests. They say that later in the night when the revelry was in full swing some dancing guest would fall in the fountain splashing water and fish on the floor.

The woman we'd rescued was waiting for us in the company of a slick blond.

The table was laid lavishly with black caviar, oysters, smoked sturgeon, cold appetizers platters, vodka, cognac and a bottle of champagne chilling in an ice bucket and a carton of Marlboro cigarettes that were available only in the hard currency stores.

"Sit down boys." The blond welcomed us with a geisha smile.

We had a few drinks together before our charming hosts excused themselves for a few minutes.

"How much money do you have on you?" asked my friend.

There was more food on the table that we could pay for with his monthly salary and my three months stipend.

Forty minutes passed. Our waiter brought pan-fried crispy chicken tabaka. The women were still powdering their noses.

"Want anything else?" asked the waiter.

"Can you bring the bill first?" I asked.

"Let me check. I'll be back," he said.

My friend poured us another drink and said,

"When he brings the bill, I'll stay, and you'll drive to my place and my mom will give you money."

The waiter returned.

"Everything has been paid for," he said.

We continued with a feast alone for another half hour before the women came back.

"Funny way to thank us," I said.

"Sorry. We had to see some folks in the director's office."

"And who are you?"

"I am the deputy director of Valdai, and yesterday you saved me from thugs who were after our 'black cash.'"

"Black cash, wow!" said my friend. Black cash was laundered money made through cash trade, bypassing the official cash register.

"You didn't even try to scream."

"I tried to reason."

"With thugs?"

"Well, had they taken the money, I'd be in bigger trouble."

She saw my inquisitive look.

"The fellas I met with tonight wouldn't have let me get away with it. I'd have to repay all to a penny or else..."

Great, I thought. *We saved the rogues from the villains.*

***

VICTOR POGOSTIN

The two blemishes I kept

Black 'Volga' instilled both fear and contempt.

In the very first week that my shiny car was parked in our neighborhood a word 'dick' was scratched deep to the metal on the rear fender. Painting over the fender or as some body workshops suggested the whole car was out of the question. The touched-up scratch vividly visible in the sun stayed and was sold with the car ten years later.

Soon a higher automobile authority inflicted the other blemish. In those days my wife and I lived in a small bachelor apartment close to the Leningradsky highway -the only direct route to my Institute via downtown. From early Spring to late Fall, between 9 to 10 am the highway was blocked to all traffic clearing the way for the motorcade of Andrei Kirilenko, Member of the Political Bureau of the Communist Party going from his dacha to work.

One warm late May morning at about 9:30, I drove to the bridge connecting my side street and Leningradsky highway. Usually, if Kirilenko's motorcade was expected, police car blocked the pass under the bridge, but this time it was clear, and I started on an empty highway towards downtown. In a few minutes, when I was passing a stalled bus, in my rear-view mirror I saw two blinding headlights of the huge Politburo limo nicknamed *Chlenovoz* or 'member carrier' (literally, dick-carrier) fast approaching my car. *Damn it,* I thought, *he hasn't passed yet.* With the trolleybus on my right, I could not hug the curb. 'Chlenovoz' whizzed by, but for a second, I blocked the path of its KGB escort Volga. When it caught up with me the window opened and an arm holding a metal rod reached out towards my car, hit my left front fender with a heavy blow, and zoomed away after its 'master.'

In about half mile the traffic police blocked me.

I stopped and walked to the police car.

The officer had his radio transmitter on, and I heard an angry voice ordering him to check my papers.

"Look what they've done," I said pointing to the dent on the fender. The officer took my driver's license, reported its number to the guy on the radio, walked me a few meters away from his vehicle and whispered: "I don't know who you are, but if you can complain, do it. We've had it up to here with them."

Flabbergasted, I said nothing. That other blemish I also kept as a souvenir. It, too, was sold with the car ten years later.

***

VICTOR POGOSTIN

Back door shopping

"I've had enough of your House of Cinema." The supermarket manager with a beehive hairstyle brushed me off. The Central House of Cinema was an exclusive creative club of Moscow cinematographers, where film screenings and festivals and other events were held. With that verdict I was cut off from back door shopping in one of the best Moscow supermarkets.

Aside from soiled vegetables, stripped-to-the-bone meat and cheap kielbasa, not much was available even in Moscow supermarkets and grocery stores. In mid and late 80s even, bakeries had queues for bread two to three hours long. People who had access to passes and tickets to theatres and creative clubs 'traded' them for the access to the back door shopping. Luckily another opportunity was not long in coming. Our new neighbor turned out to be the Deputy Director of a large supermarket on the outskirts of Moscow.

This time we traded services. I would meet her after the night shifts and make sure she safely got home, and she'd walk me through her basement pantries. At times it felt awkward buying salamis, carbonates (smoked) sausage, imported cheese and deficient candies in the underground cellars while regular shoppers rummaged through the empty counters or elbowed over the carts with cheap sausage.

This feeling of uneasiness passed quickly when I reminded myself of the canteens, special stores and food distributors services for the Communist Party and Government high brass. At least in my neighbor's pantries I paid full price, not the peanuts it cost to the nomenklatura.

***

Butcher-Matador

I think it was in the book of Vietnamese fairy tales that I read about a character that became a butcher when his father, one of the King's men, had fallen off the King's favor and the family lost everything.

Well, butchers in Russia proved otherwise. Russian butchers could get you access to the best theatres, doctors as well as lawyers and even prosecutors and judges ready to solve your problems. Much loved meat was hard to get even if you had money to buy it.

One winter Sunday my wife said that our neighbor walking her dog early morning saw a refrigerator truck unloading meat at the nearby grocery store. The word spread quickly and soon I stood in the long line at the meat corner of the store. The pallets behind the grimy glass of the counter were still empty. The only indicator that meat would soon be sold was a sign '2 kilos per customer' pinned to the poster with a cow-shaped cut-chart.

"Kolya, damn it. Soon?" shouted the salesgirl into the lift window.

"Chopping. Count twenty people and cut the line."

Not my day. I was twenty-second in line, but

giving up wasn't my way. Luckily the line in the nearby 'alcoholic beverages' store was only one hour long and soon I was in the back yard of the grocery store armed with a bottle of Stolichnaya. The sacred door to the butcher's basement was easy to find. A policeman guarded the rusty iron door.

His job was to stop the uninvited and inspect the bags of the back door shoppers.

"I am Kolya's friend," I said.

The officer pounded on the door and shouted, "It is for you, Kolya."

The basement smelled of freshly cut meat and burning fat.

Two men in stained leather aprons sat at the low table by the improvised electric stove. Two huge T-bone steaks sizzled in a frying pan. The butcher's cleaver was stuck in the chopping block next to an already open and started bottle of vodka. One of the men was reading a book.

"Who are you?" he asked.

I put my Stoli on the table.

"Good call," he said. "But still?"

He closed the book and looked at me with suspicion.

The book's cover looked familiar. It was my translation of Hemingway's *The Garden of Eden and The Dangerous Summer* fresh from the Progress Publishing House and not yet available in bookstores.

"Want me to sign it?" I asked.

"Look, buddy Hem himself showed up," he said, laughing.

I opened the title page with my name.

He moved one more stool to the table and gestured me to join them.

"Kolya," he said.

We shook hands. Another glass appeared on the table.

"Like it?" I asked pointing to the book.

"Not the Garden of Eden parts... all that love," he said, pouring vodka into tall glasses, "Bull fighting...that's tight. To Matadors, bottoms up." We clinked glasses.

"Ever seen the fight?" he asked.

"Once in Portugal," I said, "but they don't kill bulls there."

"Funny," he said. "We do and cows too."

"At least you always win," I said. "There, the bulls win from time to time."

Another T-bone steak was thrown on the pan. The day crept on and so did the life stories and toasts. Finally, he led me to a thick wooden counter with tenderloin pieces.

"Pick." He made a grand gesture, then wrapped the selected pieces in the old newspaper and scribbled the price on a scrap of paper.

"Call me next week," he said.

He went up the stairs to the door. It was getting dark and colder outside. The lonely policeman was still there.

Kolya tapped him on the shoulder and said, "Turn away. My buddy is leaving."

I was home late, drunk but forgiven. Sunday was wasted, but now my wife had a better understanding of the fringe benefits that come with literary work.

***

VICTOR POGOSTIN

Part Five - Health care for all

Koi pond

In my Toronto condo, on the way to the swimming pool, just behind the marble lobby, I like to stop by a large Koi Pond. For a few moments I enjoy watching the colorful fish splashing in the waterfall and then suddenly dashing away into their caves. It brings back memories from another life.

In late 70s Leonid Ilyichev, an Academician and a Deputy Minister of Foreign Relations was one of the editors of the book that our department worked on. Unlike many other high profile 'editors,' he actually wanted to review and sometimes even make changes to the text. In those winter days Ilyichev lived in the Barvikha sanatorium, a favorite resting and spa treatment spot for the high-ranking party-state nomenklatura. I visited Ilyichev there a few times.

I had to leave my car at the gatehouse where my ID had been checked by the uniformed security. Then I walked along the pine parkway past individual cottages reserved for the very top "servants of the people", and an open winter swan pond to a long three-storied Art Nouveau building of the Sanatorium. Ilyichev stayed on the second floor. It was there in the lobby between the floors that I stopped stunned by the soothing murmur of a decorative Koi Pond. *That's life!* I thought. *Well, maybe one day...*

It took Ilyichev an hour or two to review the updated text. Meanwhile, I had to hang around in the sanatorium's coffee bar. When the bar hostess was in good mood, I could buy a pack or two of Marlboro or Kent cigarettes otherwise available only in hard currency stores or even ask her to wrap up for me a few salami sandwiches that my son affectionately called "The Central Committee sausage." Prices in the bar were unbelievably low. Yet one day I felt flabbergasted.

That day our meeting was scheduled in the early afternoon and Ilyichev had suggested I had lunch in their canteen. It was after the scheduled lunchtime, and I had a table to myself by the window overlooking the swan pond. The impressive menu didn't show the prices but just reading it made me hungry. *Well*, I thought, *my taste buds will have a feast no matter what.* I ordered all the exquisite dishes on the list, starting with a smoked sturgeon appetizer and a pike soup with caviar pie and a beef stroganoff with mushrooms and an aromatic true English tea with fresh strawberries for dessert. Strawberries in winter! I felt guilty enjoying my desert and not being able to have my son and my wife join me in the feast.

Lunch over; I counted money in my wallet prepared to pay through the nose for the lavish feast. The bill completely dumbfounded me – 98 kopecks - less than $1.00 in official exchange rate of the time!

Adding insult to injury

Soon it was time to take the manuscript from Ilyichev and drive home. On the way to his Suite, I saw a door marked 'Pharmacy.'

My father needed a German-made injectable drug that his doctor knew about but refused to prescribe, as it was available at the party-state nomenklatura pharmacies only.

Encouraged by the lavish lunch I decided to try my luck again and knocked on the door. A friendly pharmacist smiled showing dimples in her cheeks.

She had the drug my father needed but was afraid to sell it.

"I'll give you a pack," she said. "And then you can get more in our main pharmacy."

She didn't have the nerve to ask me whom I was visiting.

In the lobby two heavy built men in dark navy-blue suits stopped me on my way out and escorted me to a side room.

They listened to my story and one of them said, "Keep the pack, but don't ever do it again."

***

Panangin

Drug used for treatment of cardiac insufficiency and rhythm disorders (arrhythmia) - I have a faulty memory for drugs, but this particular one still lingers in my mind.

The hospital room in the cardiology department was so tiny that when visiting I had to sit on my mom's bed. That night her roommate, an elderly woman from Tashkent put on her colorful Uzbek robe and left tactfully allowing us to be alone. We chatted about my forthcoming trip to Mexico, I helped Mom with dinner and showed her the latest pictures of my eight-month-old son, her grandson.

When I was about to leave, I thought I saw her eyes looked worried.

"Mom, I can still cancel my trip," I said.

"Not to worry," she said. "I'll wait. I won't let you down..."

On my way out I wanted to speak to her doctor, but he had already left, and so I stopped by the Head Nurse's office. It was late and the only light came from an old desk lamp. I brought her a chocolate cake and a book with my translation of Hemingway's 'Garden of Eden.'

"How is my mom?" I asked.

"Not bad," she said. "Did you speak with her

doctor?"

"He had left for the day. Why?"

"Well... she needs some drugs that we don't have."

"Can I have a prescription?"

"No. We are not allowed to prescribe drugs that are not available in pharmacies."

"What is it?"

"Panangin."

"I'll be back in a week and will get it."

She sighed.

"So bad?" I asked. "Just one week..."

"I have some," she said. "But not enough for two."

"For two?" I asked.

"For your mom and an eighteen-year-old boy. He is really bad. I have some for a week, but then..." She avoided looking at me and I didn't know what to say. I rose and left.

The Tenth World Congress of Sociology was held in Mexico City. I was going there as a translator for the Soviet Delegation. My seat on the plane was next to Gregory K., an instructor, consultant of the Department of Science and Educational Institutions of the Communist Party Central Committee. The instructor briefly lectured me on how vigilant we should be in the fight against imperialist propaganda. He especially stressed that we must watch out for 'political corpses' like Alexander Zinoviev's who may try to desecrate our bookstand and display pamphlets like 'Yawning Heights,' that lampoon the Soviet Society.

After the lecture he asked a flight attendant for brandy and mineral water and opened a blister-pack of Panangin.

"Do you suffer from cardiac insufficiency and arrhythmia?" I asked.

"Not really. My doctor said I should take it for preventive purpose."

"Where do you get it?"

"In the Central Committee Pharmacy, why?"

"My mom is in the hospital, and she needs it. Can you buy it for me and I'll pay?" I asked.

"Sorry Vic," he said swallowing a tablet. "Drugs in the Central Committee pharmacy are only for those who work there."

He drank his brandy in one gulp and settled snugly for the overnight flight.

My Mom passed away four days after my departure.

I knew it the moment my wife met me at the airport. As there were no earlier flights the funeral was postponed till the day after my return.

At the Mexico City *Mercado*, I had bought two traditional Mexican sweater-jackets, one for Mom and one for the Head Nurse. When I arrived at the hospital my mom's bed was empty with her mattress rolled up. I stopped by the doctor's and the nurse's offices, but both were gone for the day. I left the parcel with the sweater on the nurse's desk.

My Mom's never-worn sweater is with me in Toronto.

***

Part Six - Charlie Foxtrot

"He who has served in the army does not laugh at the circus" (old Russian saying)

Clusterfuck

My odyssey in the Red Army was conceived in Egypt. Something went wrong in the land of the Pharaohs and in 1972, Anwar Sadat packed off the Soviet military advisors back to their land. At the time, military translators were drafted and sent to Egypt to work with the military advisors. The returnees settled in the cushy jobs in Moscow military institutions pushing their freshly drafted brethren to the far corners of the country.

I'd have thought that there was no more need

to worry about the draft and I could return to my civil life. No such luck. A Colonel from the Draft Board explained that the Minister of Defense had signed the Draft Order and, in short, there was no turning back. "Congrats my Lieutenant!" he said and handed me my officer's ID Card.

The next day I appeared before the Medical Evaluation Board. A Duty Officer ushered me to a room where my evaluation was to begin. Bewildered I looked around. There was a rotary chair for vestibular tests and two men with white lab coats over their uniforms. I was told to make myself comfortable in the chair. One of the men put a blindfold on me and strapped me into to the chair.

The chair spun first right then left and then in circles. Finally, it stopped abruptly, the blindfold was quickly removed, straps unfastened, and I heard the command, "Open your eyes, get up and walk."

I couldn't even stand. The room was spinning, and I felt like I was flying towards the wall and would smash my head against the cast iron radiator. I gripped the armrests, but the radiator was approaching with an alarming speed. The men grabbed me and held tightly in the chair.

My bewilderment changed to sluggishness, and in that state-of-my-once-alert-mind, I was told to strip down to my underwear and ushered into the next room. Four or five physicians waited for me at their desks. Three of them I won't forget.

A hearing doctor, a babushka with a large head mirror was first. She examined my ears, ordered me to step a few feet back, and turn my back to her.

"Thirty-five," she whispered.

"Thirty-five," I whispered back submissively.

"What? Louder!" she yelled.

I returned to the table and repeated loudly: "Thirty-five."

"Good. See, you can do it when you want."

She scribbled something in her log and waved me off.

A surgeon quickly checked all my limbs, ran his fingers down my spine and commanded: "Show me your heels."

"Both?"

"Yes."

I stood up on my tiptoes.

"Are you nuts?" he said.

"You said both," I retorted.

"One after another, dummy…"

The next doctor was a sturdy looking redhead. She ordered me to turn around a few times, examined my skin all over and said: "Show me your head."

I obediently bent my head forward.

She gave me a dirty look and hissed angrily.

"Peel back your dick, idiot."

"Speak proper Russian," I snapped at her, did as requested, and left.

Long story short, my medical reports recommendation was *Fit for military service in all branches except Navy and Air Force*. And of course, my assignment order was to appear for appointment to the Personnel Department of the Northern Fleet HQ.

A week later, on a cold September morning a train with the distinctive name "Arctica", dropped me off at the Murmansk railway station. It poured. The handle on my suitcase broke. There were no cabs and I walked about a mile to the Military Commandant Office using my suitcase like an umbrella.

The Duty Officer studied my papers and shrugged in disappointment.

"Wrong place, buddy. Go to the main bus terminal and take an express up north to the Navy HQ."

I grabbed my suitcase and raised it over my head prepared to step in the rain.

"Hey, pirate." The officer handed me a roll of tape. "Make a handle for your chest."

It was late afternoon when I finally reported to the Navy HQ Personnel Department was sent to the Officers' Hostel. At dusk I walked to the shore to watch sunset.

A narrow path winding through the rocky

shoreline led me up to a cliff. Down below, a ragged submarine was bouncing on small waves. Shreds of rubber were hanging all over its carcass. It resembled a tired killer whale that had washed ashore and was waiting for a complete overhaul or a scrap dock. Somehow the sad-looking sub put me in a romantic mood.

After all, so be it, I thought.

Falling asleep I imagined myself smoking a pipe and marveling at the bright stars on the upper deck of a sailing vessel gliding in the far seas or listening to 'no shit, this really happened' tales of exotic ports in the officer's wardroom.

In the morning, my dreams of long nights under the polar or tropical stars were ruthlessly grounded.

The floors in the Personnel Department office squeaked like the deck of an old frigate. A grey-haired Captain 2nd Rank studied my file and said:

"Want a career in the Navy?"

"Why not. Sounds kind of romantic."

"Tell you what... the ships you'll be on do not enter ports. You'll need binoculars to see the land. For six months you'll be hanging out at sea, eating canned bread, drinking *shilo* (Russian naval slang for spirit diluted with water) and puking overboard."

"What are my choices?"

"I have a request from Long-Range Reconnaissance Aviation. It's closer to your home and will save you a year of service. Then you'll decide."

"Sign me up," I said.

The loop closed. I was fit for service in all branches except navy and aviation and wound up in naval aviation.

***

RUSSIAN ROULETTE

An Exemplary Garrison

"You guys luck out in the Exemplary Garrison," said a Duty Officer welcoming me when I delivered a sealed package to the Navy's HQ in Moscow.

I was put in a room for two on the third floor of the Bachelor Officers Quarters. The room had two iron beds, a small table, two nightstands and a sink. A narrow unsteady wooden walkway ran through the forest connecting the residential and the military plots. The residential section had two boiler rooms – an efficient one for the high brass and the barely breathing one for everyone else. In winter, a thick frost covered the inside of the window and the gap between the radiator and the wall. We often slept in our fur caps with earflaps settled firmly about the ears. Electric heaters didn't help much.

A few young married couples had rooms on the same floor and smart husbands brought in extra iron bed meshes and wired them to make electric room heaters. The load was too high for the circuit breakers and at night the breakers tripped with a cracking sound, shutting off the power for the whole floor. The panel was at the very end of a long corridor. In a minute or two the young wives began to grouse and then one of the more sensitive husbands would get up and jog in the cold to fix the breakers.

Summers, on the contrary, could be very hot. Water supply was available only in the early morning and evening hours. Hot water taps never saw any hot water and the bathhouse was run once a week on Sundays.

A one-storied building of the Radio-Technological Intelligence Unit was in the wooded area close to the airfield. A shallow, clean, cold and fast brook ran across the nearby glade. On hot days we would sneak out and sit naked on its sandy bottom to wash off the day's sweat.

***

Boot Camp

The Baltic Fleet naval-aviation boot camp in Pionersky (formerly German Noikuren) was in the old Luftwaffe digs. Nearby towered the remains of the country residence that once belonged to Otto von Bismarck, the 1st Chancellor of the German Empire. In 1943 the German military intelligence Abwehr used the residence for a sabotage school. Female radio operators were trained there and then were dropped behind the Soviet lines. In 1945 the northern part of the East Prussia, including Königsberg (now Kaliningrad) and the nearby towns were annexed by the Soviet Union. In 1995 the Pionersky boot camp was disbanded. Bismarck's dacha and the rundown camp were put out for sale but failed to enchant any commercial buyers. A few years later, the dacha had finally attracted a very prospective buyer and in 2011 the rebuilt dacha, now called "Yantar" (Amber) became yet another residence of the President of Russia.

After a year in the unit, I was commanded to the Pionersky boot camp. My orders were to bring a unit of fifty sailor-recruits who had completed their training to our naval aviation base.

After the punishing winter in the North, I felt enchanted by the warm and salty March breeze, the soft murmur of the waves rolling over the strikingly white sand beaches, almost touching the high dunes. It was late afternoon when I reported to the camp's duty officer. I asked when my unit would be ready for travel. The officer hesitated and advised me not to rush.

"We have an emergency here," he said.

"What happened?" I asked.

"Well," his voice turned to a whisper, "someone painted the moustache and the beard on Lenin's bust with ink. The orderly swears he didn't do it. Our political officer is investigating, and a special department officer has been called in too."

Lenin's bust, now freshly painted white, stood next to the unit's banner. Guarded day and night by an orderly.

Damn it, I thought, *what a clusterfuck. I'll be stuck here till they find who did it. If they found the "culprit", the poor guy would be lucky to get away with a severe reprimand that would stick in his file for many years. He'd never be able to enter a university or get a decent job.*

I remembered what a bombshell it was when a sailor from our intelligence unit "committed" a far less serious offence. In a letter to his folks, he called the head of the photo laboratory an asshole. The letter was intercepted by the special department officer doing the mail cover check and then passed on to the political officer with a recommendation to "take action." The order/recommendation trickled down the chain of command to the deputy regimental commander for political affairs, then to the regimental Komsomol leader and finally landed in my hands with the indisputable verdict 'expel from the Komsomol.' I ignored the 'recommendation.' The sailor got away with a warning notice.

Meanwhile, I needed a place to stay. The officers' hotel was sheltered in a ramshackle dwelling. Here and there the exterior stucco peeled off exposing the red brick walls of the old German barrack. The hotel's only room had about twenty squeaky iron beds with rolled up mattresses and smelled of dampness.

The feeling of enchantment quickly evaporated, and I decided to take my chances and find lodging in Kaliningrad.

The night closed on the city when the last suburban train from Pionersky dropped me off at the Kaliningrad North railway station. Hotel 'Moskva' was close. Before the war, the building belonged to a German insurance company. Now only two coats of arms on the facade lined with dark red clincher bricks reminded of its Teutonic past.

The Uniform Talks and a middle-aged blond behind the hotel registration counter plucked me out from the line of waiting civilians.

"Comrade Officer," she smiled showing the

hotel lodger to the waiting line, "You have a reservation."

I didn't, but quickly appreciated her offer and moved up the line.

My room on the ground floor was small but with a solid redwood bed, a wardrobe, a desk, burgundy drapes and clean linens felt like a five-star suite to me.

The hotel's restaurant was packed. For a few minutes I stood in the doorway trying to locate a table to share. Dancing couples blocked my view. When the music stopped, I heard someone calling to me:

"Hey lieu-fucking-tenant get your ass over here." The voice came from a red-faced Captain 1st rank (Commander) sitting at a table with three Captains 2nd rank (Lt. Commanders) and four loudly laughing women in their thirties.

The women happily snuggled closer to 'big stars,' making room for one more chair.

A voluptuous waitress put an extra plate and a glass and bending over me purred:

"What will Comrade Lieutenant order?"

"Hey?" One of the Lt. Commanders slapped her behind, "Can't you tell one of ours?"

"Hit it." He filled my glass to the edge with vodka and gestured to a well-laden table.

"Well," the Commander raised his glass "To our

young comrade."

Now, at a close range I noticed the 'Submarine Commander Badge' (a submarine image with a small red enamel star in the middle) on his black double-breasted uniform jacket.

We drank bottoms up.

"Naval aviation. What fleet?" asked the Commander pointing to the blue stripes on my black shoulder boards.

"Northern, long range," I said.

"Intelligence," he affirmed. "Good ... So, you know how to keep your mouth shut. Landed here?"

"Room 103."

"Buddy!" he exclaimed, raising his hands as if in a prayer. "I swear to God you were dropped from Heaven."

He caught my puzzled look.

"You'll know at the zero hour." He filled my glass again. "The first one flew by, the second wing calls...."

We drank bottoms up.

"Now to the brothers-in-arms, brothers for the night."

The last one went down bottoms up too.

Zero hour struck when the restaurant was closing, but not before the Commander got three bottles of Armenian brandy to go. At midnight, our three-sheets-to-the-wind crew hit the cold of the empty streets.

"Attention crew!" the Commander tried to speak solemnly. "Don't we brave the oceans?"

"Yes, Sir!"

"Don't we outwit the sub-chasers?"

"Yes, Sir!"

"Well, what was the combat mission for tonight?"

"Outsmart the Hotel night manager and the floor hostess and get our sweet support team to your suite, Sir."

"What's the Intel report?" He turned to one of the Lt. Commanders "Where is room 103?"

"On the ground floor, next to the fire escape stairway, Sir."

"Listen to my command! Lieutenant goes back to his room, opens the window and stands by. The rest of the crew quietly," - the women giggled -, "quietly I said, go round the corner to the Lieutenant's window and get ready to board."

My room was on the ground floor, its window rather high and away from the vigilant eyes of the night manager. One of the Lt. Commanders climbed up into my room. Then the other two pushed the giggling women up one by one till we could grab their arms and hoist them in. From my room the crew tiptoed to the fire escape stairway. The Commander got in last. Before disappearing into the stairway, he put a bottle of brandy on my desk and hugged me.

"We'll soon be out at sea," he said. "Not long, you know, but if you happen to be here in about six months, look me up."

We never met again.

It rained in the morning. In the early spring the white sands looked as grey as the sea.

The boot camp looked even less inviting than the day before. The culprit was still unidentified. The Camp's political officer threatened to contact his counterpart in our regiment and ask him to keep his eyes and ears open in case someone bragged about the incident.

Ironically, sixteen years later on a tour in the Naval Academy in Annapolis, I was reminded about this episode. Right inside Gate 1 to the Academy stands the Navy Bill, a sculpture of the Academy's bulldog mascot. The cadets rub his brass balls to a shine for good luck. Apparently, there too, the orderlies keep 24-hour watch over the mascot, but the 'culprits' are never caught.

A medium-height, broad-shouldered Petty Officer 1st Class was seconded to me. He was on the way home after the demobilization and would help on the way from the camp to the railway station in Kaliningrad and then with boarding the overnight train to Leningrad. In Leningrad the unit had to march to the Moscow Railway Station to catch the overnight Leningrad-Vorkuta train.

On our arrival in Leningrad, the Petty Officer lined the company in four columns, took his position to the left off the last line and looked cunningly at me. I bet he saw I had no experience leading the marching unit. I felt awkward but couldn't afford to lose my face.

I moved ahead of the column and barked as firmly as I could: "Follow me! Forward March!"

Surprisingly, all followed, and the unit trooped kicking the cobbles along the Ligovsky prospect. Just when I relaxed, the shrewd Petty Officer roared, "Sing!" and fifty out of tune voices burst into Katyusha.

> Apple trees and pear trees went into blooming,
> River mists began a floating flow,
> She came out and went ashore, Katyusha!
> On the lofty bank, on the steeply shore.

Out of the corner of my eye I caught mocking glances of the passers-by and, damn it, girls too.

I only felt relieved when we reached the station. The Petty Officer rounded the sailors in the far corner of the platform, saluted me and left.

From here on I was on my own. The train Leningrad-Vorkuta set off early in the evening. It stopped at our destination very early in the morning and for one minute only. All along the route station cafeterias stayed open to midnight, offering little food, but plenty of booze, a natural trap for my fun-starved boys.

The clock on the platform showed two hours before departure.

I needed to win their trust quick. I pulled aside a tough-looking guy who seemed to enjoy some respect of his comrades.

"Get me three more guys you trust," I said.

He went back to the group and pulled aside three sailors. I lined up the unit.

"Attention!" I commanded. "These four will take the bunks by the car doors, two on each side. Only they will be allowed to leave the car at the stations. If you want to buy anything in station cafeterias, ask one of them. I won't spy on you but will come and check periodically. *Hang up* at 10:30 sharp. At 5:30 a.m. all must be ready to disembark the train. Any loose cannon will go to a brig on arrival. Clear?"

"Yes, Comrade Lieutenant!"

"Good! Now, the first group of five goes to the cafeteria. You have ten minutes to wet and sweeten your dry rations."

The sailors laughed and the first group left.

When we boarded the train, I could hear bottles

tinkling in the duffel bags.

The passenger car I travelled in was right next to the sailors' car.

I got out watching the boys on all stops. Right after the 'Hang up' time, I walked through their car. Some of my tipsy seamen were still chatting, others already asleep.

The smoke-filled, beer-smelling dining car was at the very end of the train. It was packed and the only available spot was at a table with two army lieutenants and a grey-haired captain in the interior troops uniform. One of the lieutenants waved to me. I took the spot across from the captain and ordered more cold cuts and vodka to the table.

First, the small talk ran as usual - weather, dull road and our places of service. The three of them were already drunk and attention quickly shifted to me.

"Where do we fly, swim?" The captain filled the glasses and we tossed them down.

"In the North."

"Where are you bound now?"

"Taking sailors from the boot camp to our base."

"Brother! I am riding cons to the camp. Only mine already docked."

He was the senior officer in charge of the convoy taking cons to a prison camp near Vorkuta.

"Political?" I asked.

"Hell no. Thugs. These days political are called *lunatics* and end up in nuthouses. Listen, can you get me flying boots?"

"Flying anywhere?"

"Smart, yeah?" He poured our glasses to the edge.

To break up the drinking binge, I lit my pipe.

"Blue blood..." He screwed up his face. "Give me your pipe."

"Don't share the pipe, the horse and the wife with anyone."

He scowled at me.

"Listen ... you were wet behind the ears when I was a Petty Officer of a convoy unit. *The Master* (Stalin's nickname) was still with us. Our unit was transporting the *enemies of the people* in wagons to Vorkuta and then on the narrow-gauge railway to the end of the rail. From there the guards with dogs drove them on foot off-road through taiga to the camp. The lucky ones rode in sleighs, but mostly on foot. I hated doing it in summer, mosquitos and midges, you know. In winter it was ok. The guards had sheepskin coats. At night we stopped in winter huts. There was no room for jailbirds. We covered them with tarpaulin, and they cuddled under it to stay warm. Some froze stiff but not many. We'd leave the stiffs in the woods.

Reporting of the missing was strict. We had to bring their hands with personal numbers tattooed. It was easy. We did not even have to chop off hands with bayonets. You just lifted a frozen arm, shook it a little and the hand fell off with a sound of cracking icicle."

The captain paused briefly and for a few minutes stared into the darkness outside the chuckling train.

"Now." He took a deep breath. "Now it is a piece of cake, a resort. Now we have trucks. Not covered, but trucks... freezing anyway. Flying boots would have been handy. I'd trade any gun for it... American, Japanese, any..."

It was getting late. A surly waitress passing by dropped a check on our table. The army guys and I chipped in our share and rose to leave. The captain waved his hand and looked away.

I found the train manager and tried to negotiate a longer early morning stop. He promised two minutes.

The train reached our station at 5:30 a.m. sharp. It was dark and the spring fog hid the narrow platform and the one-storied station lined with the timeworn barn boards. The unit was ready, but the lock on one of the car doors jammed. I had to rush the sailors through the only door like jumping paratroopers. When the last three were at the door, the car jolted and started to move. I was the last to jump off the rapidly picking up speed train.

"Jump, Lieutenant, jump!" Two sailors, arms locked to support my fall, were running along the railway embankment. The platform was already behind.

My briefcase hit the embankment first. As soon as I saw an opening between the telegraph poles I jumped, fell onto the locked arms and together we ran a few meters to a stop.

"Will you be our commanding officer?" asked one of the sailors.

"No guys," I said. "All good things come to an end."

***

VICTOR POGOSTIN

Hands off the Epaulets

Lieutenant Stas Z., a.k.a. the beardy, was a poet and an outcast in the regiment. He refused to accept any form of military life and after weeks of futile attempts his commanding officers gave up on 'That Fucking Poet.' He was left alone, stopped showing up for any duty even for the regimental musters conducted on Mondays outside the HQ. That said it did not stop him from versifying bombast poetry about steel birds soaring in the sky. This leavened patriotism served him well after his return to civil life. He joined the Communist Party and made a career in the USSR Writers Union.

Beards were not allowed in the military, but Stas insisted he had an express permission from the Deputy Fleet Commander. I was a witness to it. We were at the Officers Mess that had a small private room for high brass. The door to the room was open revealing a tired looking Vice-Admiral lunching. Stas approached him.
"May I address you on a personal matter?"
"What's the matter, Lieutenant?"
"Can I keep my beard? I always had it. I am a poet."
The Admiral looked at him incredulously and said:
"Poet? Fuck off with your beard."
"See," Stas argued, "He said with the beard, not without."

It is mind-boggling why February 23rd was

chosen as the Soviet Army and Navy Day. Couldn't the founding fathers of the Soviet Military have chosen a nicer time of the year? February is the harshest months of all, and its havoc-wreaking blizzards carry something devilish in their wombs.

That year the celebration fell on Saturday and rivalry black navy and green army dress uniforms occupied the only two restaurants in town. Adventurous local blonds were sprinkled sparsely amidst the shining gold and silver shoulder boards.

The army had an advantage as its officers were quartered in town while the navy had nowhere to retreat. The last bus to the base was at 7 p.m. leaving them no choice but to try to get a hard-to-find room in one of the three town hotels or fall prey to the local *cougars*....

The snowstorm was just starting when Stas and I entered the restaurant. It was packed. Coming from the cold we stopped in the doorway adjusting our eyes to the heat and smoke of the long, narrow dining room.

"Hey beardy," A passing waitress pulled Stas by the sleeve. "See the table in the corner? You and your buddy are invited to join."

There were two women and a naval Captain at the table.

A brunette was happily cooing with the Captain, and Stas quickly landed next to her plump blonde friend.

Our waitress came back. The evening was still young, but she already looked tired.

"Well lads...make your order."

"How about peaches and Bourdeaux to start?" Stas tried to be funny.

"Peaches?" she said. "You already have two at your table. Think fast, I am busy."

"What do you offer?" I asked.

"Potato salad, fish or roast beef with potato and vodka or beer or both."

"That's all?"

"Well, sweetie," she smiled, "I finish at midnight."

Our appetizers, beer and vodka, came first.

"To our Day!" said the Captain. "Officers drink standing!"

The three of us stood up.

"And to love at first sight," added Stas.

We drank in one swig.

The jukebox started playing a foxtrot. Stas and the blond danced and returned panting.

After the third dance, Stas whispered in my ear, "I want to marry her."

"Really?" I asked. "Something in the air?"

"Yes." He turned to the woman. "I'll marry you."

"Oh dear." The woman seemed to melt.

This was his usual trick of winning a woman's heart.

After two more romantic dances sealed with generous toasts, his determination gained force.

"I want her to meet my parents, Vic," he said. "Will you be my witness at the wedding?" He gave me his best pitiful look.

"No problem," I said.

He nodded and rose to leave. Outside the snowstorm was in full swing. We reserved a room in the hotel 'Severniy' (Nord), and I thought we'd go there. But the 'bride' hung on to Stas.

"I live close across the park. Come darling, come..."

"You go," I said. "I'll meet you tomorrow noon at the Central Post office."

"No," insisted Stas. "You come with us."

The wind had heaped up high snowdrifts making the paths barely visible. Suddenly four men in long black sheepskin coats blocked our way.

"Vasiliy, look who the Devil sent our way. My hands are itching," one of them said.

"Birds..." Vasiliy spat in disgust. His coat opened revealing a sharp picket torn frm a wooden fence. All four had pickets concealed under the knee long coats. They moved menacingly close.

"Vic, buddy!" Stas recognized in one of them Viktor K. a fellow poet and the editor of the local magazine *North*.

Vasiliy looked familiar to me as well. I remembered seeing his face on the covers of books about the Russian North.

"Shit," the poet-editor spat. "Fucking party-pooper. We were snooping around for over an hour. Just wanted to have simple fun and knock the lights out of some fucking strangers and here you are with your ugly mug."

"I am getting married," Stas bragged.

"Fuck you. Don't waste our vodka buzz."

They pushed Stas aside and left.

The 'bride' lived in a small, dark log-house barely visible behind the snowdrifts. Feeble yellowish light flickered in the frosted windows. The house was at the dead end of a narrow street backing into an old cemetery, its rickety crosses barely visible in the snowfall.

Inside it was warm. The room was small and sparsely furnished – an old sideboard with plates and cups, a wrinkled black leather sofa bed and a Russian masonry stove. We hung our coats and dress uniform jackets to dry by the stove. The 'bride' brought a bottle of moonshine, and we drank to their happy thereafter.

Soon the young couple settled comfortably on the sofa, and I climbed onto a high stove bench, drew a cotton partition, and fell asleep lulled by the snowstorm and the soft sweet murmur of Stas cooing with his love-at-first-sight pitch.

A loud bang on the window made us jump in beds.

The 'bride' tiptoed to the window and looked back at us terrified.

"My husband," she whispered and crossed herself.

"Who?" Stas sat up on the sofa, flabbergasted.

"Husband, you fool. Get out fast."

"How?" I asked. "He is at your door."

"Back door...," she pleaded.

"To the cemetery? No way." Stas said.

"My God... My God. He said he'd be at the field training for three days. He is a tanker. Just get out fast."

"Field training on February 23?" I said sarcastically.

Bangs on the window became more demanding.

"Just get the fuck out," she shrieked.

"Non-flying weather, dear," I said. "Stas, buddy, shall we take the fight? After all he is not on a tank."

We were lacing our boots when we heard the front door ripped off the hinges and a tall, hefty army Captain burst into the room.

He stood still for a minute or two, then shook off snow from his hat and overcoat and plopped on a stool.

"Dammit!" He looked heavily at his wife.

"I know nothing," mumbled the woman. "I was with Varia and her friend and these two tagged along and wouldn't leave."

She grabbed Stas's jacket by the shoulder straps and almost tossed it out the window when a solid punch threw her back on the sofa.

"Don't you dare touch the epaulets, bitch," roared the Captain. "You didn't award it."

He turned to us.

"What were you drinking?"

Stas reached for the moonshine bottle.

"Not this shit," he said. "Find a real drink, slut."

The woman searched in the cupboard and produced a bottle of Bulgarian brandy. The Captain poured three tall glasses.

"To the Army and Navy Day! Officers drink standing!" he said.

The three of us stood up and drank with a gulp.

"Any grub?" he asked the woman.

She didn't answer and sat sobbing.

"What are the guys like you doing here? Listen... I know a good place. Girls...top-notch," said the Captain.

He poured the remaining brandy in glasses and threw the bottle on the sofa.

"Last one for the road and let's go."

Outside the snowstorm had changed to a blizzard. You couldn't see anything ten meters ahead.

Fighting the headwind and snow we walked to the main street and then split trying to catch a cab on either side of the street. In about thirty minutes I was lucky to stop one.

"Let's pick up my buddies on the other side." I said to the cabbie.

He made a U turn. Neither Stas nor the Captain was to be seen. We drove a hundred yards both ways. Not a soul.

"Take me to 'Severnaya'," I said.

In the hotel the room was cold.

"We had a burst pipe, and the radiators were drained out," said an old woman who let me in. "There is a cast-iron stove and firewood in the room."

At night I lay in bed looking at the primitive wall frescoes with bears and other Russian fairy tale heroes dancing in the flickering light from the dying stove fire. I thought about Stas enjoying the company of the 'top-notch' girls or perhaps still wandering in the blizzard deluded by the ingenious tank maneuver of the Captain.

***

VICTOR POGOSTIN

In The Land of The Flawed

In early May, snow was only starting to melt. Dark ugly snowdrifts piled along the garrisons' sidewalks, but in the woods the snow was still dazzling white. The orderly column of two in black and gold dress uniforms marched up the wooden walk towards the garrison's cemetery, stumbled over the rusty railings surrounding the tombstones, and broke into small groups.

After the Victory Day parade, we marched to the cemetery to remember the crews killed in crashes. Supply Unit Sailors carried several cases of vodka and boxes with small sandwiches – buttered dark rye bread with a slice of herring. In the middle of the cemetery stood a tall Stelae monument with a faded inscription "To Comrades-in-Arms" followed by a long list of barely readable names and dates. We gathered around the Stelae. Colonel said a few words muffled by the soft rustling of the wind swaying the tops of the fir trees. We raised glasses and drank in silence without clinking.

There is nothing drearier than the daily grind of the Garrison life. That Friday I was the head of the garrison patrol. Late evening, we stopped to warm at the Duty Officer's office. My patrol sailors settled down for a nap in the barrack's empty bunks.

The telephone rang at midnight. A sobbing

woman asked for help. Her daughter's boyfriend, a warrant officer from the construction battalion, came to their home for the weekend. "We treated him like a king," she sobbed. "But the moron went wild, beat us up, and kicked out the window in the hut. He fell asleep but promised to kill us and burn the hut when he wakes up."

Later that night it froze and a snow blizzard hit. When we left the garrison, the country road and the fields were completely hidden from view under a lumpy white blanket of fragile ice and snow. Soon our truck slid into a roadside ditch and bogged down in the slush.

"Comrade Lieutenant," the driver said apologizing, "I have a towrope."

"Who will tow? You? Where is the village?"

"There."

He pointed towards a barely visible copse of trees.

Groping for the road in the dark was senseless.

I told the patrol sailors to stay in the truck's cabin and went straight across the field towards the copse. The ice crust was thin, and I kept falling through it up to my ankles into water-filled furrows. I was at the edge of the copse when I heard a high-pitched barking behind my back. A pack of six foxes, their eyes glowing yellow in the dark, watched me. The pack stopped at a safe distance waiting for me to fall.

"Fuck you. I am not your prey." I yelled at the top of my voice and the timid foxes backed off a few yards.

Behind the copse, the field sloped down towards a village. The blizzard stopped. In the moonlight I could see the white roofs of the char-colored huts and barely noticeable smoke coming from chimneys. The village was asleep. Not even a glimpse of light could be discerned in the low windows.

I was passing a barn when a large furry ball rolled out onto the street and started moving in my direction. I remembered stories about a rouge bear seen recently close to the base. The barn was on the lee side of the moving ball. I pressed my back against the barn wall. I thought my black overcoat would be imperceptible against the black logs.

Pistol in hand I stood motionless watching the approaching beast. When the ball was about fifteen meters away, I cocked the pistol and barked: "Halt! I will shoot!"

The ball stopped and mumbled: "Sweetie... It's me."

The black sheepskin coat swung open revealing a babushka with a huge moonshine bottle under her armpit.

"Me who?" I demanded firmly trying to hide my

embarrassment.

"Baba Katia. It was I who called. Come...Masha is in the hut, shit-scared."

"First, get me a tractor."

"Sure, sure..., our tractor driver is there too."

I followed her to the hut behind the barn. In the passage a strong smell of cheap moonshine, salted cucumbers and sour cabbage hit my nose. The room was poorly lit and cold. The only window was smashed, and the hole was plugged with an old pillow.

The Warrant Officer menacingly snored on the warm Russian stove bench right under the portrait of Yuri Gagarin, pinned to a wooden wall. Masha sat nearby. When Baba Katia joined her, I saw that both had shiners under their eyes. A tractor driver was dozing at the table. He stared at me.

"Drink with me, Lieutenant," he said.

"Can't."

"Squeamish? Want you sailors pulled out or not?"

He poured two glasses. The moonshine smelled awful. I gulped it quick. He pulled on his wadded jacket and left.

Shortly, my chilled-to-the-bone sailors came in.

Angry, they went straight to the Warrant Officer.

"Can we grab him and leave, Comrade Lieutenant?"

"Get warm and dry yourself up first."

Fussy Baba Katia put a plate with potato and pickles and two glasses of moonshine in front of them.

"Comrade Lieutenant?" They looked at me.

"Don't," I said. "Just rub your feet with it."

A clock on the wall cuckooed twice.

I turned to women: "Wake him up and get his coat. We are leaving."

They didn't move and began to cry.

"What now?"

"Don't arrest him, Comrade Officer... He is a kind guy, when sober."

"Didn't you call for help?"

"I did... Forgive me," said Baba Katia.

"Seriously?"

The women started squawking at the top of their lungs. Irritated I ordered my patrolmen to grab the guy when the door opened and a Captain from the construction battalion entered the room.

"Shut up!" He hushed the women, then, pointing to their shiners, chuckled, "He's a real sharpshooter... isn't he?"

Then he turned to me.

"Listen buddy." He poured me a glass of moonshine. "Do me a solid. Leave him. He is my buddy too."

I put the still-full glass aside.

"Sure? What if he makes good on his threat?"

"He won't. I promise."

"What if they call again?"

"They won't."

"We won't... we won't," sobbed the women.

"Screw you all... Tell your driver to lead the way back. He can come for you later."

The Captain nodded.

My disgruntled sailors refused to move.

"Leave him," I said. "We won't be back no matter what. In the land of the flawed, the moron is king."

***

Autopilot

At the Monday regimental musters, when the sailors were marched to their barracks, and the regimental Chief of Staff asked his age-old question of "who drops cigarette butts in the HQ's urinals?", the Colonel turned to the officers: "Comrades! Sons! I inspected some of the rooms in the officers' quarters and," he paused and shook his head as if in disbelief, "and... I ask you not as your Commander but as your father... please hold the vodka stockpiles you have for March the 8th, the International Women's Day for the V-day Holidays in May."

NATO naval exercises began right after the International Women's Day holiday and our unit worked late hours. There were several workstations in the room and at night when we listened to the tapes, we could see our reflections in the window.

My immediate superior Captain Gennady R—ko pattered me on the shoulder and gestured to me to come to his office. It was nothing unusual. God knows why he had chosen me when he felt an urge to drink and spill his guts. He got drunk quickly and the subsequent guts-spilling often ended with muted "fuck Brezhnev and this shitty system."

In his office all was set for a 'heart-to-heart' conversation – sliced cooled salo (Russian lard) on thickly cut dark rye bread, homemade pickles and a large onion bulb cut in half.

"Fresh!" He smiled pointing to a small canister with pure spirit. "A gift from the Maintenance unit."

He poured two tall glasses, equal to five shots each.

"To strong-willed men," he said.

We inhaled, held our breath, drank it in one shot without breathing, slowly exhaled through the nose, sniffed the dark rye bread and took bites of lard and pickle.

Pleasant warmth spread over my body.

"Now," I said. "Shoot... what happened?"

"Not much. You will get ten days in a Brig for being absent without leave."

"And you didn't put in a word for me?"

"How come? I know nothing."

"Seriously? Wasn't it you who said I could leave without a formal request, and you'd have me covered?"

"Don't start," he said. "Sink or swim."

"When?"

"As soon as the NATO exercise is over."

"Like hell you will."

"Wanna bet?"

"Case of vodka?"

"You got it."

We drank another glass and shook hands.

It had happened in late February. One of my friends was getting married and asked me to be his best man. The wedding was in Leningrad. I needed five days for travel and submitted a formal leave request to Captain Gennady R—ko. From him it was to go up the chain of command to the Head of the Regimental Intelligence and then to the Chief of Staff.

"To hell with formalities," said Gennady. "Go. I'll cover you if need be. Bring me a bottle of good Brandy. Promise?"

I promised and Friday night took an overnight train to Leningrad and, as was agreed with Gennady, a week later I came back with a bottle of French Brandy for him.

"Save the bottle to yourself," ny roommate said.

"What happened?"

"They were looking for you all week."

"Why?"

"There was a mock alert on Saturday morning right after you left."

"Shit... and what did our Captain tell them?"

"Nothing. He too didn't show up. A foot messenger was sent for him, but he was drunk and couldn't put two words together, then they sent for you."

I went to Gennady. He shrugged his shoulders

and said that no one would help a drowning man but himself.

As per regulations a commanding officer had thirty days to put his subordinate in the Brig. After that the arrest was either nullified or transferred to the commanding officer himself. Luckily, the NATO Naval exercise lasted for over three weeks and ended on the 29th day after my arrest was formally announced. That very day Captain Gennady R—ko called me: "Get ready." He sounded as if he'd won a lottery. "Tomorrow is the Day!"

"On the very last day! No way!" I burst out.

"No worries," he said. "It's only ten days and then I'll drive you to the village and you'll buy me a case of vodka."

Making him fail was a matter of principle for me.

I planned his defeat very carefully. My first visit was to my buddy, the Chief of the Brig.

The Brig was in a small brick outbuilding with two cells painted dark gloomy blue – a large one with four beds for sailors and a single cell for officers.

I was straight to the point: "Do you want two bottles of vodka?"

"You bet!" he said. "What should I do?"

"Tomorrow my fucking chief will escort me here. Make sure I won't be locked up. I must hold out one day."

"Don't fret," he said. "Just drag it to after lunch. I leave at five."

Next day I reported to the regimental HQ at nine. Capt. Gennady R—ko was an hour late.

"Let's go," he said rubbing his hands with a grin.

"Hold your horses. I left my toothbrush and a shaver in the room."

He walked me back to the Officers' Quarters. Once in the room, I set on my bed and started coughing. My face turned red.

"What now," he asked.

"I think I have a fever."

He was skeptical, but we walked to the Medical Unit offices, anyhow.

At the Medical Unit there were two officers ahead of us and by the time a nurse took my temperature it was lunchtime. There were no more excuses up my sleeve and at about three in the afternoon we reported to the Chief of the Brig. He took his time studying the arrest injunction.

"You should have called me yesterday or early morning," he told the Captain. "The officers' cell is unavailable. I already have a warrant officer in, and his time ends tomorrow."

"Get one more bed till tomorrow," said Gennady. "A big gun like him can share the cell with a warrant officer for one night."

"Can't," the Chief of the Brig said. "Regulations!"

"Sure," I said. "I'll complain all the way up to the Fleet's Commander".

The Captain's face turned red. He grabbed the injunction and rushed back to the HQ. When he returned it was 4:30 PM.

"Here!" he said triumphantly and produced the early release order for the warrant officer, signed and sealed.

My heart sank. I felt defeated.

"Too late," said the Chief of the Brig. "I don't have a clean set of linens and the laundry is closed. Come back tomorrow morning."

A fresh set of linen for an officer was the regulation's requirement as well. The Chief of the Brig earned his two bottles.

At least one promise Gennady held. In the morning he drove me to the village store and helped to load a case of vodka in the trunk of his battered Lada. Two bottles I took to my room and set aside for my buddy in the Brig. With eight bottles left, a drinking spree started in that most favorite bar for all Russian men – a garage.

My roommate and another Intelligence unit Captain joined. Then another officer joined in and contributed a tin of sardines in oil. Gennady opened it with a rusty screwdriver and thoughtfully noted that the fatty acid was good for our blood pressure. After the second bottle I suggested we relocate to his flat.

"We'll sit at a table like normal people and cook something hot," I said. All agreed. The day was young, and we had a long way to go.

Gennady's wife had left him many years ago and he lived alone in a bachelor apartment. It had a kitchen and a table and even a bathroom with a large cast-iron bathtub. As hot water was never available, he used to store homemade pickles in the bath. "Help yourself," he offered us to fish for the dark green crisp beauties as the toasts came along.

I had lost count of drinks when a thought sobered me up, or at least I believed it had. I remembered that my friend whose wedding I travelled to was due to defend his PhD in Chemistry that very day.

"Sorry guys," I said. "I must go to the Post office, but I'll be back."

Last thing I remembered was how I was lacing my boots.

Next morning, I woke up in my room recalling nothing. My roommate wasn't in yet and I lay in my bed listening to the wet snow drumming on my window trying to recall yesterday's events. Suddenly a sharp thought made me jump in bed. *What a* shame, I thought. *I forgot to congratulate my friend.*

I got up, walked to the Post office and placed a call to Moscow. Luckily my friend answered.

"Forgive me," I said. "I am a swine. I didn't call you yesterday."

There was silence on the other end. Then he said: "Are you kidding me? You called yesterday and held me up on the phone for nearly half an hour saying only 'congrats my friend,' and I'd say, 'thank you' and you'd repeat your congrats over and over and then you hung up."

"Well." I said. "Have I? Now you know what the autopilots are for."

***

VICTOR POGOSTIN

RUSSIAN ROULETTE

Part Seven – Disenchantment

One night back in 1987 I was working at home translating Hemingway's novel The Garden of Eden. *My wife Natasha was busy preparing dinner. Out of the corner of my eye, I noticed my seven-year-old son George crouching in the hallway past my tiny study to the kitchen. He was holding my passport behind his back. "Mom!" I heard him whisper in surprise, "Daddy is a Jew?"*

My son, like my elder brother and I, grew up in an assimilated family. My parents were nonreligious, and ethnicity had never been the subject of family conversations. As a teenager I had not encountered what many friends of mine rightfully called 'domestic' anti-Semitism. Perhaps, it was our last name Pogostin that sounds like a very Old Russian surname that confused the anti-Semites. Apparently, it confused the vigilant personnel department officers too.

Anyhow, my first brush with the latent state-anti-Semitism occurred later when I was making my life and career decisions.

Religious identity was a taboo in the Soviet society. For a member of Komsomol, a political youth organization in the Soviet Union, and all youth had to join the Young Communist League at school when they turned fourteen, even attending a service in any place of worship could result in expulsion from school and make it almost impossible to enter a college or university.

I was twenty-nine when I visited the Moscow Choral Synagogue for the first time.

I was on my pre-demobilization leave and still wore my naval officer's uniform.

On a chilly October night, I was working in the archive of the Soviet Sport Newspaper. Its old-world charm building was in the Bolshoi Spasoglinishevsky Lane practically next door to the Synagogue. It was dark when I finished my work and came outside. To my surprise, the cozy inner yard was packed with soldiers. It was drizzling and the soldiers' faces were hidden under the raincoat hoods pulled up and over their helmets. Only a few hours earlier, the inner yard had looked peaceful and deserted. Stunned, I approached a stumpy short man who looked like an officer.

"What's going on here?" I asked.

"Jews are partying." He pointed in the direction of the synagogue.

"Think of it!" I said. "It may be dangerous."

"Tell me about it," he said, my sarcastic remark lost on him.

"Why're you here?" I asked.

"Just in case.... We don't have our orders yet."

I left my uniform jacket and officer's cap in the car, put on a sweater, walked to the Synagogue and for a good hour stood in the doorway admiring a group of dancing, merry men.

But let's go back to my school years.

An alarming signal from the future

In 1960 to avoid the newly introduced eleven-year schooling, I, like many of my peers, quit my secondary school, got a job as an electric fitter apprentice and enrolled in the night School for Working Youth. True, two years of working experience before the University gave an added advantage for admission.

The night school was in the building of the Faculty of Chemistry, built in the style of the Stalinist Empire (or Soviet monumental classicism), on the new campus of the Moscow State University spread along a steep bank of the Moskva (Moscow) River.

I was the youngest in my class. Most of my classmates came to school after army service, and many were married. Despite the age difference they treated me well and even protected me in occasional brawls that erupted when the male half of the class ventured out to the 'late-night dance floors' in public parks. My secondary education was inextricably linked to my drinking education. 'Blue-collars' had thirst not only for knowledge but for booze too. The Faculty's cafeteria sold nothing but bad coffee latte, cheap lollipops, sandwiches with shriveled cheese and beer. At the last recess, the male half of the class used to relocate to the cafeteria. On the New Year's Eve celebration party, vodka was poured in the beer mugs that we hid under the table from the vigilant eyes of the Schoolmistress. The effect was literally staggering. I stood against the nearest marble column in the hall, pressing my nape against cold stone. I was the only one who could stand upright. All my elder buddies were propped up by their dance partners. The Schoolmistress assumed I could help her to put the things in order.

"Pogostin," she said gripping my elbow, "take that man out." She pointed to my desk partner, a former paratrooper who'd lost his bearings on the dance floor.

"Right away," I said, trying not to breathe on her. I went outside, slid down the icy steps of the Faculty and stuffed my head into a fresh snowdrift. It sobered me up. Then I went back, grabbed the paratrooper, and supporting one another we left the hall. Our Schoolmistress had trusted in me ever since.

In the country of the Dictatorship of the Proletariat, the personnel officers of the elite Institute of International Relations (MGIMO) sought out the working youth schools for potential applicants. The communist state was trying to dilute the thick ranks of nomenklatura offspring with the working-class youth. I was in grade ten when they came to my school.

"Hey guys, let me through." The last recess was almost over, and our Schoolmistress was making her way in the crowded corridor. She stopped by the door to my class.

"Pogostin." She called me out in her husky voice. "After class meet me in my office."

"What have I done?" I asked defensively.

"You rascal!" she said laughing, "Nothing this time. Get cleaned up and don't be late."

"Well," said the Schoolmistress when I came into her office, "Comrades from the Personnel Department of the Institute for International Relations want to meet you. I think you fit the bill."

Two tightly-buttoned comrades offered me a chair at the end of a long table and asked me to briefly introduce myself and fill in the form with my personal information.

"Good to see young workers doing well at school," said one of them.

"Especially those with a good old Russian name," added the other.

He put the form in his black binder, shook my hand as if the deal was done and added: "You'll hear from us in a week or two."

I never heard from them. A month passed and I asked the Schoolmistress how things were with my diplomatic career. She muttered something about my nationality and suggested I talked to my father.

My father was old school. He'd embraced the Bolshevik Revolution in his early 20s. Indeed, the Revolution helped the Jewish youth to escape the bleak life inside the Pale of Settlement, a western region of the Russian Empire with varying borders that existed from 1791 to 1917 in which permanent residency by Jews was allowed and beyond which Jewish residency, permanent or temporary, was mostly forbidden.

His career was shaped before the war when anti-Semitism was at its low point. He had held medium- to high-level jobs in the energy industry and in the '60s was a Chief Engineer of a large Energy Trust.

In fact, my parents for many years felt a part of things. Both, however, were disenchanted with the system in the last chapter of their life.

My father's briefing on the 'social puberty' in the Soviet environment was not particularly encouraging.

"Look son," he said. "Set yourself a high goal and keep going. Regrettably, this 'nationality' shit will be underhandedly thrown at you but keep going. I won't always be there to shield you."

Thus, at sixteen, I learned that my prime challenge in life was my nationality.

My Soviet Universities

Resentment against the MGIMO personnel officers gnawed at me, so I decided to enroll in the Faculty of Translation of the Moscow State Institute of Foreign Languages (now the Moscow State Linguistic University). The Faculty was born on February 17, 1942, with the purpose of training foreign language specialists for the Red Army. After the war, in 1945, graduates and faculty members worked as translators at the 1945 Nuremberg Trials, and at the 1946 Tokyo International Tribunal. Until the mid '70s only male applicants could apply.

None of my relatives believed that a Jewish boy would be accepted. But I was.

Good entrance exam marks, new rules that offered enrollment advantages to young workers, and, last but not least, the recommendation of the district Komsomol Committee helped. The Komsomol leader at a mechanical plant where I'd worked for two years arranged for the recommendation. Not that I was an active member of the Komsomol, but rather he and his buddies were indebted to me. I was fifteen when I came to the plant and was the only one who was not searched at the checkpoint. My witty Komsomol bosses quickly figured it out and, used me to smuggle beer and vodka into the shop.

    Like all freshmen back in Soviet days, my studies began with a month-long potato harvest trip to a collective farm. The farm had an old school that looked like a shipwreck with wide cracks in the board walls, boarded-up windows and rusty roofing sheets that at night howled plaintively in the wind. Even in its heyday, the school had only one classroom. We divided it with an imaginary line into a living and dining room where we put a long, crude wooden table and benches and a no-beds bedroom with a straw covered floor. September nights were cold and to stay warm we'd throw our quilted jackets on the straw and slept in our clothes. A pit latrine was in the far corner of the thorny bush undergrowth, deep in the schoolyard. At night if you wanted to take a leak you crouched just outside in the dark. Flashlights woke up otherwise sleepy cockroaches and they scattered on the walls.

Dry law was formally announced, but not enforced and one rainy night a bottle or two appeared at our boiled potato and canned-meat dinner. Tongues wagged, jokes were swapped – from girls to different nationalities, and then out of the blue one of my new buddies, a former cadet, Alex, blurted out "Why all Jews are such rogues?"

Silence fell.

"Have you ever met a Jew?" I asked.

Alex thought for a moment and said, "Not really."

Upon our return to Moscow Alex was appointed Group Leader. One day he brought us library registration forms to fill. I checked all required boxes including 'your nationality.' From the corner of my eye, I noticed how Alex lingered on my card.

His new friend was that first Jew he had finally met. He blushed but said nothing. Next morning, he took me aside.

"Vic," he said and blushed again. "Back there at the farm I said something stupid. Please forgive me."

We have been friends ever since.

A period of relative calm

The next four undergraduate years made me temporarily forget that my 'nationality' mattered much. Then, the time came for the internship abroad. It was part of the educational process at the Faculty of Translation. My initiation to the process began with an excellent formal presentation by the Faculty Deputy Dean to a group of personnel department reps who came to select translators for their Foreign Staff Directorates. Four of the attending reps asked me to fill in the job application form and be ready for soon departure.

A month passed. My friends were packing their bags for work in the Soviet Foreign Missions, and I was left out. This time, my father's involvement helped. One of his friends from university days was now a Head of the Foreign Staff Directorate within the Ministry of Energy and my father asked him to consider me.

In late December 1966 I left for India to work for the Soviet Trade Mission energy group and returned from my internship in March of 1968. Ahead for me was one more academic year, at the end of which I was to appear before the Commission for the placement of young specialists graduating from daytime higher educational institutions. The Commission's decision was equally binding for graduates and employers.

Breaking of diplomatic relations with Israel that followed the Six-Day War in June of 1967 gave the latent Anti-Semitism a fresh impetus. The running joke in Personnel Departments was 'how to tell a Zionist from a Jew? A Jew is an employee already working in our organization and a Zionist is a Jew seeking employment.'

Whenever I inquired about employment opportunity, I was first greeted with open arms and flimsy excuses for not hiring me followed later, after I filled in my Job Application Sheet.

Note - all official forms in the Soviet Union, even library registration cards, medical records and school class registers had the proverbial *fifth paragraph* - 'Your nationality,' i.e., what certain ethnic group you belong to.

A despairing blow

Was it my Russian sounding surname that lulled the vigilance of the Institute's Personnel Department Head? Or perhaps he was too busy to go over my file, but he had done, perhaps unwittingly, a disservice to me.

Shortly after my return from India, he invited me to his office. Like many Personnel Department Heads, he was an ex-military type. A tall heavily built man with a dent in his forehead - a long-healed wound perhaps, or a birthmark - he was wearing a civilian suit, but his Lieutenant Colonel of the Air Force uniform was proudly displayed on a rack behind his desk.

"Well, Victor," he said. "The assessment of your work in India looks good. What are your plans for the future?"

I told him I loved writing and my cherished dream was to be a journalist – perhaps even a foreign correspondent.

"Great!" he said. "I have a request from TASS (Telegraph Agency of the Soviet Union) for a trainee journalist internship with subsequent job placement. Interested?"

"You bet!" I blurted out.

Next morning at the appointed time I reported to the Head of the Personnel Department of TASS. A smiling, outwardly charming man opened the sealed envelope with my file. His eyes scanned it, for a second his eyes rested on my personal data and then still smiling he welcomed me to the Department of the Near and Middle East and South Asia of the Main Editorial Office of Foreign Information. From January to June 1969, I thoroughly enjoyed my internship and prospects for my future looked great.

My intern supervisor was Vladimir K., an intelligent and knowledgeable journalist. I guess I was a quick leaner and soon I was trusted with signing off and posting information in a special Bulletin. That Bulletin included foreign information for official use and was sent to the subscribing public agencies and newspapers.

In late May, it was time to get a letter from TASS confirming my employment offer.

The letter was required for the Young Specialists Distribution Commission at my Institute. I turned to Vladimir.

"No problem, Vic," he said. "I think you did great. Come with me."

I followed him to the office of Alexander S., the Head of the Department.

"No problem, Victor," said Alexander. "Wait here. I'll go down to the Personnel Department and get you the letter."

I waited outside his office. Thirty minutes passed, but the always-punctual Alexander K. didn't return. Well, I thought, perhaps he was waiting for the Head of the Personnel Department. When an hour passed, a sickening premonition that something wasn't right began to creep in. He showed up in about two hours, walked past me and from the look on his face I knew that was it.

He called Vladimir in his office. I was invited in about ten minutes.

Grey-haired Alexander stood by the window at the end of his large office. He avoided my eye. Vladimir did the talking.

"Sorry Vic," he said, "We have a problem. The Personnel Department would have given you the letter if your second language was Urdu not Italian."

"Didn't they know it six months ago?" I asked.

"Well...it is what it is," he said. "I'll see you outside in a minute."

"Listen," I said when Vladimir came out. "If what they said is true, I'll learn Urdu and will be back in a year. If it's a pretext, tell me now so I don't waste my time."

He hesitated for a moment and said, "Don't waste your time."

I felt miserable. At the Institute, a much less friendly, irritable, skinny man replaced the Head of the Institute's Personnel Department. There was no one to turn to but my father.

He called his old friend and a long time TASS staffer. He was no less than one of the Deputy General Directors of TASS. Jewish too, he was in charge of the internal operations.

"Come," said my father's friend, "I'd rather not do it over the phone."

We went to his place. He and my father had a long conversation, but all I remembered was my father's friend saying, "Misha, they won't even hire *my* son."

The trouble has come, open the gate

In the meantime, there were more blows coming my way.

After my return from India in March of 1968, I had the whole spring and summer before beginning of my last school year. I used my free time working short assignments as interpreter. Students of the Faculty were prohibited from soliciting assignments or job offers individually. In fact, as freshmen we had to sign pledges that we wouldn't have contacts with foreigners outside the official assignments approved by the Dean's office. Most of my assignments were in the Foreign Commission of the Writers Union, The Academy of Sciences and the Soviet Peace Committee. I had good reviews of my work from all three and I tried the Writers Union First. They had no staff openings at the time, but vaguely hinted that I could try again if all other options failed.

The Peace Committee Personnel Department was happy to offer me employment, but only prior to getting my filled job application form that featured my nationality. One excuse followed another until I stopped calling.

In the Foreign Relations Department of the Academy of Sciences the HR officer who handled my brief interpretation assignments said they had already submitted a few requests to our Distribution Commission and assured me that he'd choose me at the Commission meeting.

All prospects for the pre-approved distribution

had to be confirmed by Georgy Yudintsev, one of the Deputy Deans of the Faculty of Translation. I informed him about my meeting at the Academy.

The Commission met for three days. The list of the invited graduates was posted on its door, and we had to strictly follow the order in the list. When it was my turn Yudintsev appeared at the door and physically stopped me from entering the room.

"But it is my turn," I said.

"Here, I decide whose turn it is," said Yudintsev and called out another graduate.

That day I wasn't called in. When the Commission members were about to leave for the day, I asked the Academy rep if his offer was still standing.

"Sorry Victor," he said. "Comrade Yudintsev said you have accepted a different job offer and suggested another graduate."

I went back to the Writers Union. Valentin K., a literary translator and a Deputy Executive Secretary of the Foreign Commission, knew me well and offered a gentleman's agreement: to ward off the undesired distribution order, he would give me a formal personal request for the Distribution Commission and hire me as an extra-budgetary staff member at the Department of Reception of Foreign Delegations. For my part, I had to give him my word not to insist on the permanent position, something I could have tried as the decisions of the

Commission were legally binding.

Yudintsev refused to honor the request.

"You will accept what we have for you," he said.

His desk was outside of the office of the Faculty Dean, and I knocked on the door.

"What are you doing?" Yudintsev yelled, angrily trying to stop me. Too late.

"Come in." I heard the Dean's booming voices.

Our Dean, Valentin Kuznetsov, a military translator in the past, a colonel (reserve) with deep rolling bass and an excellent military bearing was highly respected among students.

"Ok, shoot," he said when I closed the door behind me.

I briefed him about my ordeal.

"Gotcha," he said. "Wait outside and tell Yudintsev to come in."

For a few minutes I could hear the Dean's angry roar. Then Yudintsev came out. His face was red and not looking at me he signed the Writers Union request.

The extra budgetary staff member position helped, but only temporarily.

I had to start building my life. All my buddies from the Faculty had been assigned cushy positions in foreign relations departments of various governmental and public organizations.

My friend Alex was offered job at TASS. He

declined.

"Why me?" he sincerely wondered, "Why not you? You like writing, you have published articles, and you after all had their internship?" Even one of my closest friends who had become a Head of the International News Desk at one of the national newspapers confessed to me that his Editor-in-Chief had told him he wouldn't dare hiring a Jew.

I didn't want my former classmates to feel sorry for me and stopped seeing them.

Charting a new course...
An old man in a black jacket decorated with an impressive service ribbon looked at me from an old photograph pinned on a rustic wall.

"Is this your father?" I asked my cousin.

"Yes, retired."

I came to my cousin's dacha for a family dinner. Back in the 1950s he had gone through a similar ordeal and now had some words of wisdom for me. The cousin graduated from secondary school with a silver medal, but the International Relations Institute's Admissions Committee refused to accept his admission application. Then his father a colonel in the Border Troops put on his ceremonial uniform heavily decorated with orders and medals and went to see the Chair of the Committee.

"I heard you don't accept applications from

Jews?" he asked bluntly.

"It's a bunch of lies." The Chair of the Committee tried to look genuinely surprised. "What's your son's name?" He wrote the name down and added. "Tell your boy to come and see me."

My cousin was admitted. He graduated with Honors and was sent to the Central Post Office to perlustrate personal correspondence. A few years later he accepted a junior teaching position at a distant periphery college, defended his PhD thesis, and ten years later returned to Moscow.

"Want my advice?" he said. "Don't fight windmills. Land any job at any Academic institute, enroll in a post-graduate school, defend your thesis and opportunities might open."

He contacted his friend who worked at the newly-created Institute of Sociological Research.

A few days later I had my job interview with Fyodor Burlatsky (Soviet political scientist, journalist, publicist) who at the time was the Deputy Director of the Institute. He offered me the position of a Junior Scientific and Technical Assistant. It was the lowest research position in the Academy, something like a laboratory assistant. I accepted.

Burlatsky handed me a blank sheet of paper and said, "Write an employment application." Then he wrote "Hire" in the upper right corner, signed it, and said: "Now, take it to the Personnel Department and call me if there is a problem." There was none.

After less than two years at the Institute of Sociology I was drafted and paid my dues as an intelligence unit officer of the Long-Range Naval Reconnaissance Aviation of the Northern Fleet.

A month prior to being transferred to reserve I once again tried to fight the windmills.

Clad in my black and gold naval officer uniform, I knocked on the doors of two largest news agencies.

First, I was back at TASS. A policeman at the main entrance saluted me, a Personnel Department officer welcomed me with a broad smile but having closely reviewed my application form, sighed sympathetically and said: "Why on earth have you taken your mother's nationality? Did she insist?"

Poor chap couldn't even imagine that Pogostin could be a Jewish name. He scribbled 'Russian' next to my father's name and said: "Call me in a week. I'll see what I can do."

He could do nothing.

Next was the Novosti Press Agency (APN). There the reception was even more cordial. The Head of the Personnel Department didn't waste time. He called in the Head of one of the

Departments that had an immediate opening and bubbling with joy over his find of a young Naval Officer with knowledge of two foreign languages suggested I filled in the job application form right off the bat.

"Sure," I said. "I'll bring it next week."

"Why wait," he said and patted me on the shoulder. "I'll be off for a quick lunch, and you make yourself comfortable in my chair and fill in the form."

I did and this time my 'Sorry, but no' came in a very sophisticated way. First, I was asked to reconnect in about a week, then in a month as the Chair of the Agency was on vacation and finally, he said something that completely baffled me: "Know what," he said, "Get married first and then we'll circle it back."

I was back to the 'stop fighting the windmills' advice.

After demobilization I returned to the Institute of Sociology, enrolled in the extramural postgraduate program at the Moscow State University School of Journalism and defended my PhD thesis on Hemingway's nonfiction.

Interestingly, Yassen Zassoursky, the Dean of the School of Journalism and my thesis adviser helped me in the same way as Fyodor Burlatsky. I came to Professor Zassoursky to enquire about admission to the post-graduate school. All I had to prove my credentials was a few published articles and translations. Zassoursky never asked to see my personal profile form. After the interview he signed my admission application and told me to take it to the Personnel Department.

I worked at the Institute, attended the post-graduate course at night and above all built a career in literary translation. My new resume broke the ring of isolation, in part self-imposed, and I reconnected with my Institute buddies.

My father passed two months prior to the day I was to defend my dissertation.

Even in the last chapter of his life, he tried to find excuses to reconciliate with the failing social system.

"You are almost there," he told me once. "Turn the page of the past over."

Sorry, Father, but I couldn't. And thank you, Father, for the lesson you gave me when I was sixteen. Much shit had been thrown at me by bully-crats, but Father, I refused to get used to the taste.

It was back in TASS when my enchantment with the system began to peter out.

***

Passage to Canada

Self-fulfilling prophecy:
It was three in the morning when a hard knock on the door made my roommate and me jump in bed. Two men burst into the Embassy hostel room. One of them beamed a flashlight in our faces and demanded to see our passports.
"Where were you last night?" he asked.
"In the movies."
"When did you return?"
"At about ten."
"Why haven't you signed for return in the departure and arrival log?"
"We forgot, sorry."
"Forget again and both of you will be sent home."
We lied. That night we secretly escaped to the Eldorado restaurant exotic dance show at the New Delhi Rajdoot Hotel.
Gardelina, a beautiful Philippine dancer swirled across the small dance floor gradually getting rid of her colorful clothes. Down to her garter and a flower garland, she danced towards our table, put her foot on my knee and offered me to roll down her stocking.
"Where are you from, Blue Eyes?" she charmed me with a seductive smile.
I was twenty-one and over a year on the strict 'no foreign women' abstinence pledge that I had to make at the briefing at the Communist Party Central Committee

prior to my departure to India. At the briefing I was warned, "Stay away from foreign women. All of them are agents-provocateurs."
It would have been unthinkable to mention the USSR.
I froze stiff, mesmerized by the slowly rolling down stocking and then blurted out 'Canada.' She threw the flower garland over my neck and ran away.
I never saw her again. But Canada, twenty years later, surfaced in the Perestroika fog.

Much has been written about the gradual collapse of the Soviet system, and Perestroika of the late '80s that put the final nail in the system's coffin. The Soviet media, however, continued with creative tales of how to make it more (sic!) efficient to better meet the needs of people. In those days, a popular joke read, 'If you are hungry don't open your fridge, instead turn on your radio or TV.'

Chronic food and consumer goods shortages was nothing new to the citizens, especially in the province. In the 70s the slogans all over Moscow were "Let's turn Moscow into an exemplary communist City." Back then I was in the military and stationed not far from Vologda, the city traditionally associated with its butter and lace. Lace was available only in the Beriozka hard currency stores in Moscow and I had never seen butter in the city's groceries. Officers could buy half a kilo (about a pound) of butter at the Base's

Post Exchange once in two weeks and it was the best gift we could bring to the romantic dates with the city girls.

In the '80s and early '90s, food and even manufactured goods practically disappeared even in Moscow stores. Food tourism prospered – hundreds of buses carrying so called 'art and monuments lovers' from Moscow region and beyond flocked to the capital, parked in adjacent to shopping centers streets and released angry passengers to scour the store shelves. In order to cut off nonresidents from the already scanty food supplies, the Moscow government introduced a 'Buyer's Card.' The Card, a sort of voucher, had the buyer's photo, address and passport number; on the reverse side it listed the quantity of the deficient goods – like cheese and butter – one could buy per family. Muscovites had to carry passports so that their registration could be verified in the stores. Soon, the innovation *boomeranged* – the Muscovites and vouchers were introduced in other cities and towns of the country.

In June of 1990, my wife Natasha, our ten-year-old son George and I ventured out on a river cruise into the wilds of what was at the time hungry and troubled hinterland of Russia. Not to mention, the Captain of the thirty-year-old 'Alexander Pirogov' passenger ship, but even the cabin boy who checked our tickets on the ladder was three sheets to the wind.

"Do you want me to cancel the trip?" I asked my wife.

"Please don't," pleaded George.

We went aboard and the fun began.

The *Buyer's Cards*, that limited the non-Muscovites in their shopping rights, backfired on us during the trip.

The night of departure my son said that he had left his toothbrush home. "No worries," I said. "We'll buy it at the first stop."

The first stop was in Uglich; a one-thousand-year-old town haunted by the terrible story of the stabbing death of an eight-year-old Tsarevich (Prince) Dmitry, the youngest son of Ivan the Terrible.

It rained heavily all morning. The town and the nearby coastal villages sprinkled in the uncharted Volga banks shrugged hiding under their tin roofs every living thing. The rain turned to drizzle only when our ship docked by the long squeaky pier. Was it the gloomy weather or the gloomy history of the place, but everything about it – the rain-washed path that led past the blue-domed Church of St. Dmitry on the Blood and up to deserted streets lined with time-worn low houses with attics looked depressing?

We found a toothbrush in a small variety store. I went to the cashier to pay, and she refused to sell it.

"Are you local?" She looked at us with suspicion.

"We are from the ship," I said.

"Muscovites?"

"Yes."

"You won't let us shop in Moscow and we won't sell to you here."

It took me about twenty minutes to convince the store manager that my ten-year-old son was not responsible for the Moscow government decisions. Finally, an exception was made – George returned on board triumphantly holding a new toothbrush.

The victory was short-lived. In a few days our ship made a sharp right turn into the Oka River, the largest tributary of the Volga, and soon moored in another history rich town of Murom. After a few hours of touring the ancient monasteries, we wanted to buy something to diversify our boring boat menu. Tough luck: stale bread and dusty fish cans in the grocery stores, lonely sunflower seeds and potato on the abandoned coarse wooden stalls of the farmers' market. Next door to the pier we stopped at the 'Vodnik' (Water-Transport) store. Surprisingly, in the far corner, next to the shelves with Turkish tea in packets, we came across a counter with condensed coffee and milk, canned braised beef and Chinese ham. George wanted condensed coffee and Natasha was tempted by condensed milk. Amazed by such abundance, I was about to pay when I noticed a sign 'Sold for special coupons only to boat crews.' All our arguments failed to produce any effect on the salesgirl, and we left empty handed.

Back on board I tried to get help from our First Mate.

"Forget it," he said. "It's not for us either. It's for the cargo ship crews, but even they need special coupons valid for one month only." He looked around to make sure that no one was listening and added, "Even if you want to live in Russia, you can't."

In the fall of 1989 the imminent economic collapse, rampant crime, premonition of civil war made immigration the talk of the day. Most of our friends had left or were about to leave the country, some to the States, and others to Germany or Israel. Concerned, mostly for our son's future, we too decided to explore immigration opportunities. Both my wife and I were fluent in English and the obvious choice would have been America or Canada.

We had neither close relatives nor friends who could sponsor or help with a job offer.

My mother once mentioned that her cousins moved to Canada in the 1930s, but all she knew was the surname and she showed me a few old photographs of the family.

At the time my only contact and friend in

Canada was Al Purdy. Back in 1975 I was his and Ralph Gustafson's interpreter and travel companion in their trip to the USSR on the invitation of the Soviet Writer's Union. Al and I corresponded for many years and exchanged gifts. Al sent me pipe tobacco and I reciprocated with Cuban cigars, but Al was a poet, not a researcher and he failed to find my great uncle, a needle in the Canadian listings haystacks. Our prospects to start a new life and provide our son with a better future looked hopeless.

The winter of 1990 was harsh and brutal and that February morning the weather was particularly bitter. I was working in my tiny study when the phone rang. Natasha answered the call. The new Director of my Institute asked for help with interpretation at the afternoon meeting with two executives from the American Jewish Committee. I gestured that I wasn't available.

"Why?" asked my wife when she hung up.

"Too cold and I have work to do," I said. "And he didn't like my recent article."

"So, what" she insisted, "help not him, but the two Americans. They've come from so far away."

"It's freezing outside. The car won't start." I tried to shirk.

"Try," she said. I went.

The Institute of Sociology where I had been working for almost twenty years was falling apart. It couldn't even pay its electricity bills and the remaining researchers worked in half-empty offices with winter coats draped over their shoulders warming themselves up with hot tea, chess and political jokes like 'what will be after perestroika? – a shootout and then a census.'

The only heated floor was the Administration one. Two gentlemen, both named David, one from the AJCommittee Executive Branch and the other Director of its Institute of Human Research came with a hard currency lifeline. They offered to conduct a joint survey on Anti-Semitism in the Soviet Union. The topic had been a taboo since the establishment of the USSR in the early 1920s. The meeting went well and ended with signing of the Letter of Intent. We shook hands and the Americans left.

I went to our accounting to get the latest salary, and then stopped by my department to have tea and laughs with my colleagues. In about forty or fifty minutes I returned to my car, dove around the Institute and having broken through a roadside snowdrift came to the street almost next to both Davids. Dressed New York-style in light demi-season coats, their noses blue from the cold, they were still hoping to catch a cab. I stopped and let them in.

"Where do you want to go?" I asked.

"Nearest subway station or the Embassy, if it's on your way."

"No problem," I said. "It is halfway to my home."

We were close to the Embassy when one of them asked: "Victor, are you Jewish?"

"Yes. Why?"

"What are you doing in this Godforsaken place?" asked David from the AJCommittee.

"What are my choices?" I asked. "One should have relatives or some kind of a hook to get out."

"All Jews have relatives somewhere in the world. Don't you?" said David from the Human Research Institute.

"I do, in fact," I said, and I told them what I heard from my mother about her cousins in Canada and the photographs they gave her on departure.

In the rear-view mirror, I saw the two Davids look at each other.

"What else do you know about them?"

"Not much. My mother mentioned she heard that they had settled in Montreal and her cousin Joe had four sons."

For a few moments there was silence in the car.

"Look Victor," I heard one of them say. "We think we may know the family and if they are your relatives consider your troubles over. Write a letter to Joe, make copies of the photographs and bring them tomorrow to our Hotel. We fly back day after tomorrow and we'll contact the family. If they think you are related, they'll get in touch with you."

March, April and May passed, and we stopped hoping when the letter "Dear Victor, I am Joe..." came. It was filled with heartfelt emotions and had Joe's mailing address and his Montreal phone number. In mid June I was to go to New York to translate for a group of Russian businessmen looking for opportunities in the Promised Land. I called Joe from my room in the Barbizon Hotel. Joe said he and his wife would come to New York.

The cozy lobby was packed with tourists from the just arrived in Montreal buses. In the midst of the noisy crowd, I spotted a couple quietly sitting on a red velvet bench near a coffee shop. The old man's face resembled the wrinkled face of my mother.

"Joe?" I asked approaching.

"Victor!" the old man rose and gave me a hug.

That June my four-year-long saga of relocating to Canada began.

***

RUSSIAN ROULETTE

Acknowledgements

I want to start by thanking my wife, Natasha and my son, George, for inspiring me to write my stories and for their patience and advice on the early drafts.
Also, I want to thank Phil Rudolf and
Terry Blechman for being my first and encouraging audience.
And I would like to thank my editor, Garry Somers, who saw merit in my stories.

About the Author: Victor Pogostin was born in Moscow. He graduated from The School of Translators of the Moscow State Institute for Foreign Languages, worked as translator for the Soviet Trade Mission in India, taught Russian Language and Culture course at the Aligarh Muslim University, served in the Long Range Naval Reconnaissance Aviation of the Northern Fleet. After his return from military service defended his PhD dissertation on Ernest Hemingway's Nonfiction. For many years he worked in the Institute of Sociology of the USSR Academy of Sciences, while working as a freelance author/translator for national newspapers and literary magazines throughout the former Soviet Union. In addition to translating fiction and nonfiction into Russian, he has compiled, edited, and written introductions and commentaries for over a dozen books by North American authors, including the works of Ernest Hemingway and John Steinbeck. In 1993 he relocated to Canada with his wife and son. In Canada he worked in senior executive positions for Companies doing business in Russia and for the past seventeen years in the conference production industry. In English his non-fiction has appeared in The National Post (Canada), Canadian Literature magazine, Russian Life magazine (Vermont), The Epoch Times (US & Canada editions), "As You Were: The Military Review. Vol.14, 2021" (US), The Blotter Magazine (US) and The Other Side of Hope magazine (UK)

VICTOR POGOSTIN

RUSSIAN ROULETTE

www.ingramcontent.com/pod-product-compliance
Lightning Source LLC
Chambersburg PA
CBHW051752040426
42446CB00007B/336